TO EVEREST VIA ANTARCTICA

Thirty-seven-year-old Robert Mads Anderson, now living in New Zealand, began climbing twenty-two years ago in his native state of Colorado, in the United States. He has now climbed all over the world, including seven expeditions to Mt Everest. In 1988 he led a four-man team that succeeded in making the first ascent of a new route on the notorious Kangshung Face without oxygen.

He moved to New Zealand to live in 1983. He is a former advertising copywriter and a widely published author and photographer whose work has appeared in books, magazines and newspapers internationally.

In September 1991 Anderson set out to accomplish a world first, the solo ascent of each of the world's seven summits, the tallest peak on each of the world's seven continents. This book is about that journey.

TO EVEREST VIA ANTARCTICA

CLIMBING SOLO ON THE HIGHEST PEAK ON EACH OF THE WORLD'S SEVEN CONTINENTS

Robert Mads Anderson

SWAN·HILL
PRESS

To Margaret-Anne Seddon

Copyright © 1995 Robert Mads Anderson

First published in the UK in 1996 by Swan Hill Press,
an imprint of Airlife Publishing Ltd
in association with David Bateman Ltd, Auckland, New Zealand

First published in New Zealand by Penguin Books Ltd

British Library Cataloguing in Publication Data
A catalogue record for this book is available from the British Library

ISBN 1 85310 820 0

Printed in Hong Kong

Swan Hill Press
an imprint of Airlife Publishing Ltd
101 Longden Road, Shrewsbury SY3 9EB, England

FOREWORD

Robert Anderson is like the great wandering albatross drifting around the world and popping up in unexpected places. Over the years we have met frequently — at an American Alpine Club function in New York; at the 40th Anniversary of the first ascent of Mt Everest in London; and of course in Auckland, his adopted home. In 1993 he almost reached the summit of Mt Everest alone and without oxygen. The next thing I heard he had been surfing on Australia's Gold Coast south of Brisbane and got hit in the eye by a rogue surf board! For some weeks he suffered double vision.

Robert has always been a formidable and innovative climber. As a youngster he started his mountaineering in Colorado and then spread his activities to the European and New Zealand Alps and to the Himalayas. It was his sharp eye that saw an almost impossible route through the tortuous East Face of Mt Everest — and in 1988 his small team pioneered a way up it and put a man on the summit of the world.

He is never short of ideas and has a remarkable ability to gain corporate support for his programmes. In particular, he enjoys solo attempts on great mountains. He has climbed Mt Aconcagua in South America solo and reached the top of Mt McKinley in Alaska too. He has climbed Mt Elbrus, the highest peak in Europe, and made two ascents of the Vinson Massif, the tallest mountain on the remote Antarctic continent.

So life for Robert Anderson has never been dull. There are always great adventures to undertake, expeditions to organise and funds to be raised — and he is rather good at doing all of them. Sometimes he doesn't reach his objectives, and he has been harassed with terrible weather and nipped by frostbite. But he always comes back for more; he is a very determined performer. His story will undoubtedly make very good reading.

Sir Edmund Hillary

PEAKS
OF THE
SEVEN SUMMITS

AUSTRALIA
Mt Kosciusko
2,230 metres (7,316 feet)

SOUTH AMERICA
Mt Aconcagua
6,960 metres (22,834 feet)

AFRICA
Mt Kilimanjaro
5,894 metres (19,340 feet)

NORTH AMERICA
Mt McKinley
6,193 metres (20,320 feet)

EUROPE
Mt Elbrus
5,633 metres (18,482 feet)

ANTARCTICA
Mt Vinson
5,140 metres (16,864 feet)

ASIA
Mt Everest
8,848 metres (29,028 feet)

CONTENTS

IV
NORTH AMERICA

V
EUROPE

VI
ANTARCTICA

VII
ASIA

APPENDIX

ACKNOWLEDGEMENTS

LEARNING THE LACK OF LEOPARD LOGIC

IT WASN'T UNTIL I DESCENDED from Kilimanjaro, riding along a dusty road in East Africa, that the first good leopard story surfaced. Iain Allen, mountain guide and author of the official guide to Kilimanjaro, was piloting his Peugeot 504 down the dusty track, baboons on one side of the road, giraffes on the other.

'The big cats look for patterns when they hunt. We were trapped in our tent on the south side of Kilimanjaro with a leopard circling. We spent the night making different noises, clapping and singing, banging the tent, to keep it away. Once a leopard has established a pattern in its prey, they attack, so we always had to vary the noise. We put our one ice axe between us and each kept a hand on it. Whoever the leopard went for first, the other would grab the axe and try to stab it. We were up all night. Being a nocturnal hunter, it finally just drifted away in the morning. A Japanese man had disappeared in the area just prior to our visit. He wouldn't have known how the big cats hunt to a pattern.'

It was patterns I'd been looking for to reach the top of the Seven Summits, the similarities that would link the peaks of the world's continents together. But this had been nothing more than animal instinct, hunting summits, hoping one would be enough like the last, to sneak up, follow the plan, reach the top and be gone. Having stood on the top of three continents with the completion of Kilimanjaro, I felt Iain's leopard logic encapsulated what I'd learned to avoid in order to be successful. An animal instinct may have been what was easiest, but it wasn't the best way to approach the

1

cultures or the climbs. What the continents had in common was far less important than what was different. To be successful on the peaks it was more important to learn intuitively and adapt to the new cultures and climbing conditions, than to ascend relying on past experience. I'd be better off lacking in leopard logic, discarding learned patterns to continuously challenge myself with the new conditions I encountered.

This is what had drawn me into rock climbing in the first place. It was like gymnastics without rehearsal, every move a new challenge, relying as much on physical as on mental agility. Growing up in Colorado, day after day had been spent on the cliffs above Boulder, swinging up the arête of the Naked Edge, over the roof of Kloberdanz and sleeping in hammocks hanging from the side of the Diamond. In 1977 I was off to visit relatives in Norway and discovered the added pleasure of first ascents, climbing high above the fjords by the light of the midnight sun, the tranquil setting balanced by fierce black cliffs arcing up into the clouds, trolls hiding in the forests below.

Following sojourns to Europe and South America, and armed with a degree in writing eventually collected after studies in outdoor leadership in Arizona, literature in London and pottery in Washington State, I set out to bicycle around the world. My third stop was New Zealand. Feeling immediately at home amongst the people and the mountains, tired of travel, broke, and as friends later pointed out, with a flat tyre on my bicycle, I landed a job as a writer in an advertising agency. The qualities that had got me up the cliffs seemed to apply equally well to business and soon I was managing an office, which led me to start my own company in partnership with Daryl Hughes. Clients included BMW, Fay Richwhite, Roche and Sheraton Hotels. Building the business was accomplished by what Warren Buffet, the multi-billionaire American investor who had his own way of explaining leopard logic, paraphrased as, 'Studying history isn't a good way to succeed at business. If it was, we'd have librarians running Fortune 500 companies and I don't know one that is.'

During this time I'd been to Beijing and secured a permit for the Kangshung Face on Everest. In 1988, with Paul Teare, Ed Webster and Stephen Venables, I completed the first ascent of a new route, climbing without oxygen. Stephen Venables summited on 12 May, 1988. In Lhasa, Tibet, following the expedition, I met Reinhold Messner, the first and only person to solo Everest. While much had been written about his physical attributes, it was immediately apparent that his real strength was his mental acuity, his ability to think quickly and react to situations as they developed. His experience and knowledge was formidable, but his greatest asset was looking forward, not back, not letting the patterns of leopard logic impede him in his ascents.

From a climber's point of view, the Seven Summits aren't technically difficult, so I didn't have any desire to complete a number of long hikes and snow stomps. But most of the peaks offered more challenging and steeper routes to the top. Wherever I could find a more difficult or steeper route that suited a soloist, I'd take that. Climbing alone would increase the challenge but would also allow me to climb much quicker than a group of climbers. I'd be able to attempt peaks from lower camps and climb without tents, sleeping bags, stoves and food that weigh so many climbers down. This would make the climbing more fun, moving quickly up steep routes on each continent's tallest peak. It would also be something that no one in the world had done before.

'Solo' in the simplest terms meant climbing alone without any outside assistance. As there are no set rules, I would start where the climbing started and ascend without assistance to the summit. On some peaks, like Mt Elbrus in Europe, the start was defined by a high camp and the ascent would be little different from any other, as the slopes of the volcano offered no more than a variation on a theme from any side and everyone who ascends it is faced with much the same challenge. But in North and South America, Antarctica, and climbing without oxygen on the North Face of Everest, the climbs are far more remote and committing, making soloing an exciting proposition.

Soloing also meant the relationship I had with the peaks was not one that would be overshadowed by a climbing partner. So many climbs are ruled more by the human than the natural element. By climbing alone, I'd be exposed only to the mountain and the emotions it evoked. In my travels, though, I'd not be entirely alone, as Joe Blackburn would be accompanying me to shoot video of our journeys and, in a more enthusiastic moment, partner me to the top of McKinley, on my second ascent after completing the solo.

The success on Everest's Kangshung Face introduced me to the benefits of linking mountaineering to sponsorship, so I formed a foundation that two years later, with the sale of the advertising agency, allowed me the time and resources to set out on the Seven Summits Solo. Along the way, it would have been easy to review previous ascents, tick off summits ascended and feel the next one would be similar or even easier, a pattern to be followed, a success to be copied. But that wasn't the point.

The only way to ascend the Seven Summits, or undertake any challenge, is to define yourself by where you are going, not where you have been. This limits an adventure only to what you can dream up. In the end I experienced far more in the reality of the Seven Summits Solo than my early dreams led me to believe. In the pages to follow, perhaps some of these adventures will inspire a few more dreamers to set out on their own, looking forward, not back, and completely lacking in leopard logic.

I
AUSTRALIA

CHAPTER 1

EVEREST ALONE

THE ONLY REASON I wanted to ascend the lowest of the Seven Summits, Mt Kosciusko in Australia, was because of what had happened on the North Face of Everest four months previously.

Everest came alive as I dozed. The crevasses around me cracked, the wind howled between the ice towers, the snow whispered in sullen murmurs and the ghosts of dead climbers crept out to crowd around my tent. The lost souls on Everest were frozen but never slept. With 6,700 metres of oxygen deprivation, my blood turned to chilled mud and left logic frozen. The link to the spirit world was the only avenue in the brain that was still frost-free.

The world below — the world of live people and warmth and air — became dream-like. I floated with goblins and ghosts, talking and singing. Sleep was without rest, a haze of nightmares seen through icy skeletons. At midnight the goblins were dispersed with a lighted candle and the friendly roar of the stove. At 2 a.m., outside the tent, the air was so crisp and cold the crampons could shatter the ice beneath my feet and bring the stars down on my head. The moon was a streetlight as I started up Everest: two kilometres of vertical to ascend on a face five kilometres across. Climbing above camp was a joy after the coffin-like confines of the tent. But three crevasses loomed before the safety of the North Face was reached: the first, and I was treading an icy ridge suspended like a log over a frozen river; the second, a leap and a few gasps of 7,000-metre air to recover; and then a sugary, hole-riddled jumble at the very base of the Face with ice blocks falling off and tumbling sound-lessly into unseen depths below. Above, the ice reared, shiny, black and sinister in the moonlight.

The climbing was too consuming to be frightening, each ice axe placed with just enough of a flick to gain purchase but not shatter the ice, every foot kicked only centimetres above the last to preserve the delicate balance. The huge bulk of Everest shrunk to encompass only the next step; I crept upwards until the slope angled away, ice plated over ice like sheets of rotting glass. Five hours later and a kilometre higher I crept off the North Face and onto the windswept North Ridge. With the storm building, I continued until early afternoon, then huddled on a ledge under a rock overhang for protection from avalanches and crawled into my nylon bivouac sac. Climbing without oxygen, there was no choice but to proceed with as little weight as possible. Thus there was no tent, no sleeping bag and no rope. Only a thin, single layer of nylon made up the bed.

Within the first hour, it was obvious it wasn't warm enough. By sunset, I had been sitting on the ledge for five hours — five hours of snow flurries, mini-avalanches cascading down my back and the body growing cold and stiff. There would only be more of the same as darkness settled in. The lack of oxygen, like living with a bag over my head, the cold seeping to the core and the impossibility of lighting the stove in the rising wind, combined to create a battle to keep even the flicker of life interested. I told myself it would pass. Only the Rolex convinced me time was still moving. But its seconds felt like minutes and minutes hours as the night dragged on. I'd survived a night just as high on Everest before, on an ex-pedition up the Kangshung Face in 1988. But this cold was unique, forcing icicles into the lungs and forming a frosty fog in the air on every outward breath. The world had frozen and there was a good chance I'd soon join it.

Dawn was heralded by a smudge of grey on the far horizon of Tibet. The jet stream was shearing rocks off the ridge above and wafting them through the air like leaves. Snow was falling like an avalanche from the clouds. By the time the boots were on and I'd

7

started down, all feeling had vacated the toes. A stop to warm up would have required removing my bulky over-boots, outer boots, inner boots and two pairs of socks, exposing fingers to frostbite as well. So I kept descending, the mountain eating its cold way up my feet, while every step took me down out of the storm, away from the deathly cold and closer to the warmer, oxygen-rich tropics of the Rongbuk Glacier.

I had frostbite, there was no denying it. As a holder of only nine toes as a result of earlier adventures on Everest, I knew it would take months to heal. The question was, would a week of rest soothe the bubbling blisters and the frozen black flesh that now passed for five of the remaining toes. I was frightened of the resolve I had built up, even with my toes threatening to fall off. I had to have another try. Only the weather had defeated me and the rapid descent had saved me for another attempt. The importance of a speedy descent was brought home several days later when I learned of the fate of another soloist. Rudi Lang had reached the same height as I had and on the same day, several ridges away. But when the storm hit, he decided to wait it out. He was last seen still sitting there, frozen, a permanent fixture on Everest. There are only two types of Everest climbers — the quick, and the dead.

A week later I was back at 8,000 metres, a day away from the summit. But the wind funnelled off the North Face and roared across the ridge like a wayward freight train. I didn't even bother spending the night, descending the three kilometres of vertical and ten kilometres of horizontal down the glacier and back to Base Camp.

Base Camp was a haven of warmth and comfort after the mountain. My Sherpa cook, Passang, ensured I had three meals a day and my partner Margaret Seddon encouraged me for a final attempt. The frostbite had survived the latest sortie, admittedly not getting better but not getting any worse either. And every day later in May, the weather was a little warmer. There was one more attempt in me. The frostbite was continually painful and, since I had spent six weeks above 5,000 metres, the Everest weight loss programme had taken two stone from my body. But if the weather co-operated I knew I could reach the summit. The only way to find out was to go back up the mountain.

Living in the shadow of Everest had attuned me to the environment, and I had become more mountain creature than man. I hopped over crevasses and scaled ice walls without a second thought. Storms could be smelled in the clouds and starlight guided my skis through the glacier to the base of Everest. But Everest cared nothing for physical aptitude. All that was allowed was a simple animal-like survival set against the best training. Getting to the top would require something extra. And the right weather.

After the initial nightmares at Camp I, life up high never improved. The mental oppression of the mountain hovered about and the goblins in the wind always remained. From the disappearances of Mallory and Irving in the 1920s and Boardman and Tasker in the 1980s and the falls of soloists Roger Marshall and Michael Parmentier, the North Face of Everest emanated a dark history.

Snow beat down on the tent all night and avalanches swept over the ice cliffs above. The monsoon was threatening, and while it warmed the days, the afternoons and evenings brought heavy snow. Two days later I finally ascended through the wind and storm back into the rarefied air at 8,200 metres. The temperature hovered at minus 35 degrees Celsius. The wind tore at the tiny tent. Unable to eat and racked with nausea from lack of oxygen, I staggered out of the tent at 4 a.m. The mind led upward and slowly the body followed. Progress seemed ridiculously slow, a baby taking its first steps. Enveloped in the billowing down suit and mittens, I was isolated from the outside world. But the cold crept in, toes went numb, then feet and ankles lost feeling. The way to the summit was wreathed in cloud and wind but that wasn't the real problem — just the cold, eating away at my muscles for warmth. I rested on a rock, the summit 500 metres above and a very long ridge away. Three previous soloists had failed to reach the top and, underestimating how hard it would be to descend, had also failed to get back down alive. I could live with not getting to the top, but not with failing to return as well. The toes wouldn't last the ascent and I'd lose them, and perhaps my feet, to frostbite.

Admitting that, it was an easier decision to return to the tent. Inside, with the stove going and lukewarm tea close at hand, lethargy overwhelmed me. Movement was impossible, either up or down. My body wouldn't budge and my mind floated away. Lying there, half comatose, maybe one brain cell worked. The problem was, that brain cell still wanted to go up. So I waited out the day, praying for good weather and a temperature rise to something civilised, like 20 below. At dawn the wind was howling like a thousand demons outside the tent and inside my head. Toes refused to warm up. With weather having the final say, I started down. For three days I crept down the mountain. No slips, no slides, no rests, no sleep and, in the end, no water. Getting up had been easy compared to this. I dragged myself along like a naked brain, bouncing and banging and hauling itself over the steep rocks and ice cliffs onto the glacier far below. It had been eight long days up high and even the hallucinations and music crowding the brain didn't hold back the pain. Toes thawed with energy created by the body eating muscles. Sun and wind had burned my face to a crust and frostbite ate away at my nose. The glacier-hopping mountain creature was reduced to a stick-like automaton, the body descended only with gravity's help. The rolling glacier was a slip and slide down, then a long crawl up the smallest hills. But there was no choice.

At Advanced Base Camp, only the prayer flags remained, waving their entreaties for safe passage up the valley to the mountain. Eight days on the mountain suggested only another soloist with dreams larger than life. My companions had fled to the sanctuary of Base Camp. The following day a slow stagger took me back through the valley of rock to civilisation. I felt weary to the depths of my emaciated bones. I'd lost well over two stone, parts of my mind were lost in the haze and my feet were too tender to walk on. The summit hovered 15 kilometres away but I no longer looked at it.

My Tibetan yak herder friend Kassang was reluctant to return above camp to retrieve my skis from the glacier. 'The Yeti gets the last man on the mountain,' he said. 'You were very lucky.'

A week later we had retreated to Kathmandu. The mountain was remote. Only a lingering headache, a vagueness, a cadaverous body and black toes marked its passing. At the local climbers' café, news filtered back of a final assault on Everest by two Japanese. As the last man to the summit descended the icy ridge on his way down, the clouds closed in and he disappeared. I remembered Kassang's words. Life remained a gift.

CHAPTER 2

AUCKLAND,
BALL'S PYRAMID, SYDNEY

I RETURNED FROM Everest to Auckland, New Zealand. One day floated into the next with articles and slide shows bringing the failure to summit repeatedly to the fore. As the frostbite healed, I went back to running, looping up around the extinct volcanoes of One Tree Hill and Mt Eden, feeling the world again stretch out below me from their miniature summits. I'd wanted to start the Seven Summits with Everest. What now?

If Everest wasn't going to be the first of the Seven Summits Solo, perhaps it could be last? Maybe I needed practice. The closest of the Seven Summits, Mt Kosciusko, was only a hop over to Australia and not really a climb at all. With a wedding to go to in Sydney, the trip could extend to a loop south for a few days and a walk up the hill. It would be the dead of winter, lending about as much excitement to a 2,000-metre peak as could be expected. At least the road that led nearly to the top in summer would be closed. It never entered my head that I could fail on this, the lowest of the Seven Summits.

With Kosciusko located on the continent of Australia and a mountain called Carstenz Pyramid on an island in Indonesia, which peak was actually Australasia's highest depended on which rules geographers preferred (see Appendix). Climbers opted for Carstenz as it was far more interesting and difficult to ascend, but it wasn't really on a continent. The best answer was to climb Kosciusko now and ascend Carstenz later, just to make sure of all eight of the Seven Summits.

Auckland receded, the North Island looking long and skinny, set between the South Pacific Ocean and the Tasman Sea, a green slice on the blue of the ocean. Ten years before I'd flown over the same sea into Australia and found a flat continent that held little hope of great mountaineering conquests. In reading further, I came across the strangely named Ball's Pyramid, described as 'the world's tallest sea tower'. A fuzzy picture showed a black rock poking out of the water. Only the figures gave a clue as to its true size: 'a monolith jutting over 600 metres straight out of the sea'. It seemed like the ultimate climbing adventure in Australia, the vertical version of the Great Barrier Reef. Knowing no Australian climbers at the time I enlisted a friend, Steve Sanford, from New York; cooped up in the city after a move from Colorado, he would rapidly succumb to the adventure inherent in this discovery.

The closest point to Ball's Pyramid is tiny Lord Howe Island, several hours' flight east from Sydney. The plane, a twin-engined Beechcraft, was very weight restrictive, with a baggage allowance of 15 kilograms per passenger. The solution was to wear climbing overcoats and stuff the pockets with the heaviest of climbing equipment. Steve stepped on the scale and it shot up to 88 kilograms. The flight attendant looked suspiciously at his slight frame and the clanking overcoat. 'Climbers are often quite heavy for their size,' I volunteered, 'very dense muscles.' We snuck on the plane, pitons and carabineers tinkling quietly away in the 20-kilogram coats.

Two days later we departed Lord Howe on a chartered fishing boat. As we rounded the corner of Lord Howe, Ball's Pyramid rose like a shark's tooth from the deep blue sea. The boat crested one swell after the next, the pyramid growing until it didn't look earthly, a black castle rising in tiers straight up from the sea. As we drew closer it blocked out the sun, casting a dark shadow over the boat. Six hundred metres in print and 600 metres in reality were a long way apart. Six football fields stacked end on end straight into the sky, circled by sharks at the base. The Tasman Sea frothed in angry crashing waves, swells breaking over the rock, swirling in writhing pools of foam. What had started as a lighthearted adventure was suddenly looking deadly serious. Jumping into the frothing sea seemed suicidal. Our arrival was heralded by Steve succumbing to seasickness, leaning over the side to lose his breakfast. With my own stomach in turmoil, I was happy to depart the rolling of the fishing boat for the sea, a rope around my waist, and swam for the cliff. There was no beach or even a flat rock, just a black cliff rising straight out of the waves.

On the uplift of a large swell, I grabbed the rock and climbed up quickly to secure the rope. The boat pulled away, waves threatening to sweep it against the cliff. The rope came tight around my waist and the deck-hand held tight. For a split second I clung to the cliff, the rope ripping at my waist, knowing I was going to be dragged back down the rock and into the swell. The waves had now receded into a frothing mass of submerged rocks ten metres below on the outgoing swell. I jumped, pushing out as far as I could, hovering in the air before crashing into the sea. I went deep, feeling the water rushing past me as I plunged through the waves. One foot struck a submerged rock and my ankle twisted, tearing the ligaments and slicing open my foot. I came to the surface still attached to the rope leading to the boat, riding the swells with the surf crashing against the rocks, threatening to throw me back against the cliff. My glasses had disappeared and with them the world. A blur of big boat, crashing waves and black cliff floated past. 'Let go the rope, let go the rope,' I screamed. The deck-hand needed strangling for tearing me off the rock.

After the lucky first flawless ascent of the cliff, returning for a second try looked improbable. I drifted in the water, my foot leaving a stream of blood, pulled around behind the boat like a piece of shark bait. This was one of the most shark-infested places on earth. I swam for the cliff; the swell carried me up and back. Twice I scrabbled up the rock, only to be torn off by a higher wave, bumping and scraping my body back down the cliff into the froth. Then the swell receded. I clambered up and found a notch in the rock, wedged into it as the next wave roared over, then climbed madly for higher ground.

I was safe and Steve followed, diving into the sea between bouts of seasickness, hauled ashore on the rope like a fish. Equipment drifted in on a long line with the specially inflated kayak bags bobbing through the sea. We climbed to a large flat terrace, the sea crashing below. We'd wanted adventure in Australia, and we were being amply rewarded. We were the first two-man team to be ashore, previous ascents having all been accomplished by large expeditions. We felt stranded, the black rock a haven only for bird life and tiny scuttling lizards. There was no sign of humanity, no water and the only escape the fishing boat which could return only in good weather.

We started climbing the next day at dawn, swinging around vertical ridges, and were soon looking straight down 500 metres between our feet into the sea. We climbed over the clumsy-footed baby booby birds, already the size of full-grown turkeys, who pecked curiously at our rock shoes and chased the climbing rope. The view south was devoid of islands. The blue of the Tasman Sea extended to the horizon while grey shadows circled far below, shark fins breaking the water in crisp wakes of white.

After a night on a thin ledge, legs straddling a rocky outcrop so we didn't roll off in our sleep, the sun shot back out of the sea and heat poured back into the rock, steam flowing from the stumpy green plants clinging to the ledges. At the summit ridge, our water supply exhausted, sweat dripping from every pore, lizards eyed us suspiciously and we turned and set off as quick as we'd arrived, following the swooping sea birds down with a rush of air. The escape, a flying jump into the sea and the swim back to the fishing boat, was a leap back into real life, escaping the deserted desert isle of rock. If only Ball's Pyramid were the tallest peak in Australia!

CHAPTER 3

THE LOWEST MOUNTAIN
IN THE WORLD

ON A CONTINENT as large as Australia, you'd think the land would have had plenty of time to rise up and form a real mountain or two. Where Africa managed to squeeze the heights of Kilimanjaro out of the equator and up to nearly 6,000 metres and Asia tops the lot with Everest sitting comfortably in the jet stream at 8,848 metres, Australia, if anything, seemed to shrink from its shoreline, the land growing drier and flatter the further it got from the sea. Just finding a mountain in all that flatness could prove the biggest challenge of all.

The rental car company in Sydney pointed me towards Thredbo ski area in southern New South Wales, then slapped an extra $1,000 waiver on the insurance for 'visiting an area of potential snowfall'. It seemed danger lurked at the heart of even the most innocuous adventure.

Sydney's distinctive oystershell Opera House and fairytale harbour framed by the bridge shooting from North Sydney into the city fits neatly on souvenir tea towels, to remind tourists of just what the perfect city should look like. Having worked in a high-rise advertising agency in North Sydney with an expansive view back over the harbour, I'd spent more than one day enjoying the outlook, an ideal location for a copywriter prone to daydreaming.

The highway led south through Sydney, high-rises fading into twisting streets, as if the street plan came from London, not sure where it should take you. Red brick terrace houses fronted the road, then shops, then car lots as the red lights grew further apart and the traffic picked up speed. The Ford something or other, one of the anonymous V-8, four-door, over-sold and under-engineered cars of the 90s, floated along. Its saving grace was a powerful stereo with a search beacon that located Australian rock and roll on command. The road led towards Canberra, four lanes of 110 kilometre an hour traffic flowing through the rolling brown grass-covered hills. After New Zealand, the land felt immense, rooted to the core of the earth. Big cars and big roads and big countryside stretched out as far as the eye could see. The main road carried on to Melbourne but I turned south towards Canberra.

Canberra is custom-built, designed to house the Australian government in complete efficiency, based on a grid of concentric circles with all roads leading to Parliament. The V-8 roared in one avenue, swung through the circle and out the other, like a yo-yo on a string, gaining speed for the grand assault. Low buildings lined the broad avenues; there were smooth grass gardens behind black iron gates, gum trees rising with their shredded bark, vacuumed daily from the grass, the embassy of this and that lettered in discreet bronze on the pillars. The petrol tank must have been huge, the car swooping along with no dip in the gauge as Canberra faded in the dusk.

Three hours later the car crept through the night, surrounded by the gum trees of the Snowy Mountains. The road was a black swath of ice, and snow was pelting through the trees like falling koala bears. Maybe the extra insurance had been a good idea? It was so incongruous, this mix of tropical growth and snowstorm. The radio announcer forecast more blizzards, with rescue teams already looking for three cross-country skiers missing in the clouds that shrouded the peaks. I had to admit it, there must be a mountain here somewhere.

Base camp was the Thredbo Alpine Hotel, a fireplace-warmed mishmash of Swiss architecture, small pane windows and steeply slated roofs inhabited by enthusiastic Australians in town for Carnival Week. In the hallways, the shouts of excited revellers with a second wind after skiing moved from room to room, schnapps and hot buttered rum fuelling minds wresting every minute from their holidays. The snow fell thick and fast all night, blanketing cars and muffling the band in the bar by midnight. Sleep came quickly with the base camp comforts of white sheets and heater purring, at the foot of the lowest mountain in the world. Tomorrow was the big day, the first of the Seven Summits Solo.

At dawn the skiers' buffet, 20 metres of sausage, potatoes and eggs, warded off the effects of the night's après-ski while ensuring energy for the day ahead. Equipped from the back-country ski shop, I was carried by the high-speed quad chairlift towards the top of Australia. Strict soloist ethics demanded I chose a chair to myself, riding all alone into the perilous heights. While the weather at the bottom of the lift could have been described as threatening, at the top it had progressed to appalling. A high camp was called for, a retreat to the lift café for a hot chocolate. The temperature hovered at nine degrees below zero, the wind swung the chairs at the top of the lift like leaves and ten minutes later the lift ground to a halt. 'Closed, windy conditions.' Icicles hung from the skis, the unfamiliar bindings jammed, fingers ached with Everest aftermath sensitivity. I pointed the skis uphill and set off into the mist. An hour later, with the tips of the skis barely visible, it began to appear that, even if I reached the top, I was unlikely to know the difference! My lightweight clothing, better suited to a day's rock climbing in the sun, was suffering in the onslaught. Inside, it dripped against the skin, while ice crystals formed on the outside. The compass was unreliable, spinning in circles, negating the only way to manoeuvre in the dense cloud. I tried to remember if a compass in the southern hemisphere still pointed north. Shouldn't it point south? The brain was as cloudy as the weather. The toes still suffered the hangover effects from Everest. Even letting them begin to get cold was out of the question. Descent to camp was called for. Hesitation in the cold wasn't allowed. Cold was cold, anywhere in the world. I retreated, wandering down off the hill into a deserted ski area, the lifts closed, chairs dangling empty and ghostlike in the clouds.

Back at the Thredbo Alpine Hotel, the carnival event of the week was body painting, an exercise involving minimal clothing and maximum imagination. Tigers wandered among zebras and three people made up an elephant. A toothbrush arrived with a walking tube of toothpaste. The local paper had low-pressure circles covering the area and the ski area advertised its best snowfall in years. It didn't bode well for skiing across ten kilometres of featureless mountain to the highest point of an indistinct ridge called the top of Australia, and Carnival Week was no way to train for the perilous ascent.

I retreated to a village on the edge of the Snowy Mountains, watching the clouds roll over the peaks on the edge of town. 'Gateway to the Snowy Mountains' graced the arch welcoming me back to the Australian plains. Failing on Everest was one thing, but was I to be defeated by Kosciusko as well? The Summit Motel, a cosy retreat with licensed restaurant, loomed out of the dark. I'd hibernate for the night and let a fresh day decide my fate. At dawn I was up and out for the morning paper. The weather map held more concentric circles, the big 'L' sitting on top of Kosciusko. I was doomed. But at $26 a night I could hide at the motel until summer and the rental car company recited 'Good on ya mate!' when I called, hopefully meaning keeping the car wasn't a problem. I'd seen worse base camps, I consoled myself. I was an Everest veteran. I would not be easily deterred.

Three days and seven books later I returned to Thredbo ski area from the flats. The road was piled with snow, but the sun was bright and the sky clearing. The gum trees groaned with melting snow, their dark green leaves contrasting with the ice dripping off their branches. The final clouds broke as I rode up the chairlift, ascending 500 metres in 15 minutes, the same distance I'd missed the top of Everest by. The ridge glistened with new snow but the sky was clear as far as I could see, the heavy blue of a continent that didn't seem to know it had mountains until it snowed. Towering grey granite boulders sprouted from the featureless plateau, huddled like overgrown frozen potatoes in the morning mist. To remind of the receded blizzard, ice plastered them, as if thrown there in huge buckets, long tentacles stretching to the ground. The power of the wind had sculpted them into huge thorns, swept over the rock like a thick fur. The ice was just beginning to drip in the morning sun, like laundry hung out to dry.

The land below fanned out as the ridge rose higher, the depths of the continent rolling away, across the sheet of bright white snow to the dark blue-green of the gum trees before fading into the shadowed orange of the plains more then two kilometres below. Skis traversed the hills, gliding over the rough, hard snow. Ice-encrusted wooden poles jutted out of the snow, marking trails with no names that led in circles. Snowdrifts and cornices lurked behind huge boulders, popping randomly from the plateau. I circled the ridge and dipped through a valley. Just below the summit the snow steepened and I was forced to carefully sidestep up the bulge, the only challenge before the rounded hump of the top.

A metre-high, ice-encrusted cement pylon jutted from the snow, the top of Australia, Mt Kosciusko, all 2,230 metres of it. It had taken an hour and twenty-three minutes for the ascent. Still, it felt very much like the roof of the continent. The 360-degree panorama stretched off into the horizon. Clouds forming to the west could be traced building off the plains and swirling about the mountain, before trailing off into the east in long streamers. It certainly wasn't Everest, but it did feel like a mountain. It didn't have much to do with just getting there though, but with the hidden adventure of it, the discovery of a mountain and blizzards and ice in the heart of a desert continent. With six more summits to go, at least I had started.

I turned my skis and pointed them downhill. The air rushed past and the skis slid off the ridge and into the valley in a long sloping turn. The mountain was empty, the storms having frightened everyone back to the cities; it sloped away and then back to civilisation, dropping to the top of the chairlift at the ski area. I swooped off the plateau and into the trees, feeling the snow go from hard crust to the manicured slopes of the skiers' play areas. I'd been to the top of the continent and returned, the conquering adventurer, no lift lines for me. Forgetting my heels were loose in the cross-country skis, I ricocheted off the run into the trees and careened to an abrupt halt, upended in a snow bank.

The familiar road wound north back to Sydney, the rhythm of the drive and the stereo on seek-and-secure taking me away from the mountains. Australia had produced another adventure, a blizzard worthy of a mountain twice its height. The feeling of the summit and the Australian continent at my feet had been unique — a huge land mass with no higher place to go. What would the top of each of the continents be like, the ones that actually involved a long climb? It would be worth it to find out. One summit down, six to go.

Back in Auckland I plotted out the peaks on a big layout pad, setting a schedule for the year. Joe Blackburn, who I had worked with on Everest in 1988, phoned and said he wanted to accompany me to film and shoot photographs. It would provide company for the journey but wouldn't intrude on my climbing plans. Joe had spent seven years in the Navy, floating around as an electrical officer on nuclear submarines, before becoming a professional photographer. He had worked in Yosemite with Ansel Adams, and his photography was more art than a simple representation of the world. We'd always got on well during two previous Everest expeditions, an essential element in the time we would be spending together, while our diverse interests ensured we'd be happy exploring on our own when the opportunity arose. We set dates to meet up in New York, with our sights set first on Aconcagua in South America, closely followed by Kilimanjaro in Africa. Having discovered adventure on Kosciusko against all odds, I wanted to start seeing the world from the top of the other six continents immediately, if not sooner.

II
SOUTH AMERICA

CHAPTER 4

MADISON AVENUE TO MOUNTAIN

LONG BEFORE VISITING Aconcagua, the tallest peak in South America, I'd read an account of the first team to complete the South Face in alpine style, climbing without the fixed ropes that would have allowed them to retreat quickly from the mountain. The three climbers, trapped by a storm high on the Face and unable to retreat through the overhangs below them, could only climb higher to escape. They faced the force of the legendary 'viento blanco', the white wind, that roared onto the slopes of Aconcagua. It brought blinding snow and intense cold, wrapped them in a blizzard that howled so loudly they couldn't even hear one another screaming in the storm. On the ninth day the leader of the three left his partners lying in the snow to freeze and crawled up the final ice slopes to the pass between the summits, snuck over the ridge and down the normal route to safety.

His two fellow climbers perished on the upper reaches of the mountain, never to be seen again. The feeling of isolation, of struggling on with no hope of retreat and only difficult climbing allowing escape, had always stuck in my mind. Aconcagua emanated a unique atmosphere of fear, with climbers freezing alongside the trail of the normal route and being blown off the ridges of the more difficult routes to the summit. Underneath its sugar-frosted coating with orange and yellow rock towers shooting out of the glaciers was the whisper of death in the wind. I'd already been warned about the frozen body that lay at Camp II on the way to the summit.

Turning the corner off Madison Avenue in New York City's Upper East Side, I was pulled back from my South American day-dreams to the lecture that night at the Explorers' Club. As I looked up at the five stories squeezed into the row of houses built one on top of the other along the street, there was little to differentiate the Explorers' Club from the line of mansions it sat in.

The double iron gates nearly fill the entire width of the arched doorway. They don't squeak, but open silently, swinging on massive hinges. The wooden door inside opens only with a solid shove and the worn and polished grey stone stairs lead to the foyer. Inside, the weight of wood and stone lend an atmosphere that would be ominous, were it not for the enthusiasm of the members relating stories, mostly true and often humorous, of their latest adventure. Up the winding staircase, the heavy wooden rail leads past paintings of explorers in Antarctica and musk oxen in the Arctic. Leadlight windows look out the garden, an elevated balcony with a few large potted plants that in the confines of New York passes as a wilderness experience. The lecture room holds 100 people. I'd arrived early to make sure the projector clicked, the spare bulb was handy, the microphone wasn't of the screeching variety. Then I retreated to the Members' Bar, home of tall tales and small lockers to hold private drink supplies. Even with ten people the bar is cosy, but it easily expands to hold twice as many, perhaps from the inhabitants' experience of life in small tents.

A story of 'my personal encounter with a guanaco' surfaced as I entered, concerning the elusive breed of llama found on the slopes of Aconcagua. Conversation moved to Buenos Aires and on to Machu Picchu, Peru, before leaping back to Iguacu Falls in Northern Argentina. Seemingly the most knowledgeable man slid me his business card later. 'Just publishing a book on South America now,' he mentioned. 'Never been there myself but it's a good read. Perhaps you'd like a copy, publisher's rates, of course?'

The journey to Aconcagua started early the next morning, my birthday and the first of the big peaks coinciding. On the plane, the *USA Today* article I'd been interviewed earlier in the week for outlined the plan.

CLIMBER TACKLES SEVEN SUMMITS

Mountain climber Robert Anderson begins solo quest to scale seven world summits without oxygen.

New York, USA. 23 January, 1992. Mountain climber Robert Anderson flies to Buenos Aires, Argentina, today to begin a year long adventure to seven summits all over the world.

But what really will get Anderson's adrenalin going is his plan to summit alone and without oxygen.

'I've been on other peaks, and to do it in the standard style wouldn't be much of a challenge,' said Anderson, 33, formerly from Colorado.

His schedule: Aconcagua, South America, Feb.15; Kilimanjaro, Africa, Feb.23–March 10; Everest, Asia, April; McKinley, North America, June; Elbrus, Europe/Asia, Sept. 29–Oct. 12; Djaja in New Guinea (its continent location is disputed, but Anderson recently climbed Kosciusko, tallest peak in Australia), November; and Vinson, Antarctica, December.

Anderson has attempted to climb Mount Everest four times. He came within 300 feet of the summit in 1988, but deteriorating weather sent him back.

'Robert weighs risks,' says partner Joseph Blackburn. 'He decides the mountain will still be there.' Blackburn, 45, a New Jersey photographer, will document the odyssey and accompany Anderson most of the way up the peaks. Then, Anderson is on his own.

'When I reach the top, I will enjoy the view, say a quick prayer, then come down. I have practised taking pictures of myself,' he said.

Climbing without oxygen might be the biggest risk for Anderson, a former advertising executive.

'You have to keep going when everything in your body tells you to go down,' he said. 'You literally have to take one step and five breaths. It would not make a good movie.'

Like most press, it was largely right, but for a climbing expedition to make it from specialised journals to the general pages was always a welcome change.

At the airport in Buenos Aires, the dislocated feeling long-distance jet travel creates rose up, a New York winter and a South American summer crowded into 24 hours. Spanish was being spoken everywhere, luggage wandered off on its own and the transfer flight was at another airport miles across town. A taxi-driver in dark pants and sparkling white polyester shirt offered a 'special', smiling crookedly, a $120 fare for us and our seven bags to the domestic terminal. At the Aerolineas Argentinas transfer desk, the dark-haired, brown-eyed Spanish beauty sympathised with our plight. 'Here, put these on your bags,' she said, passing over transfer tags, 'and don't show them your tickets. You'll be there in no time.' The taxis frowned, the bags were stacked into the bus and off we roared. Better to economise; it was a lot easier to save on taxis now rather than on mules later.

The bus roared up tree-lined avenues and along motorways for over an hour to reach the domestic terminal. With a waving of arms and shrugging of shoulders the seven bags were checked to Mendoza and Joe and I retired to the restaurant for lunch and the three-hour wait in the non-air-conditioned heat of a southern hemi-sphere day. Straight off the icy streets of New York we found it smothering, hours rolling past unnoticed.

'Where have you been? We've been paging you for half an hour, the plane's gone.' Oops. My watch had been adjusted for a three-hour difference, but there were only two. The ticket agent looked at us like lost children. The use of forms always increases as efficiency decreases, so we filled out a few while we waited and officials hummed and hawed behind the counter. Taller men with extra stripes on their shoulders were consulted. Knowing looks, murmurs of 'locos gringos', pointing at watches and laughing. Another flight seemed possible, maybe now, maybe mañana (tomorrow, the Spanish language's most used word). Our luggage flew towards Mendoza while we sat in a heap of transit passengers sweating quietly.

Thumbing through 'Learn Spanish on your flight' put the troubles into perspective. The person who wrote it was desperate to get somewhere, with the first half of the book filled with, 'Help, I've been robbed,' and, 'Quick, where is the toilet?' Nowhere was the line for, 'I can't tell the time and missed my flight.' As often happens, negotiations moved from '*no possible*' to '*mañana*' to '*Rapido, rapido, aeroplano aqui*.' The flight was fixed, special forms filled out in triplicate for the transfer from one airline to another and Buenos Aires receded below our wings, a city of symmetrical streets and wide boulevards, a perfect grid from the sky. The plains stretched out below and the sun burned red over the Andes as the plane swooped towards the mountains. Two days, two airports and two beers after leaving New York we bounced into Mendoza.

'Your luggage is not here. The office is closed. *Mañana!*'

A row of unattended airline counters, a rapidly emptying airport and darkness welcomed us to Mendoza.

'Can I help?' Immediate suspicion; the day had been going too poorly to expect assistance.

'I studied viticulture in America, perhaps I can help. My name is Raoul Menendez,' he said, extending his hand. He was of medium height, with a square dark face, brown hair and eyes, the white open-neck shirt and brown polyester pants that were so common. He was of a type: slightly too eager to assist, but polite. But the luggage was lost and we needed help. Bags of video gear, solar packs, cameras and a hundred rolls of film were floating around somewhere, not to mention ice axes and double boots. It was now dark and the airport felt like a wild west outpost. Our new friend went hunting. '*Mañana*.' The luggage was somewhere, it hadn't been sent on or back as there were no more flights.

'Would you like to visit the *bodega*, my winery, in the morning?' Raoul asked. 'The airport won't be open until later, you might as well see something and it will keep your minds off the luggage. We will find it. I will collect you at eight?'

It was settled in that rush-into-the-new-land feeling that greets the traveller. Fears of being rolled for the excessive film supply and NASA-approved solar chargers diminished. He was the only person who could help with our plight. The streets of Mendoza were unlikely to yield even the heaviest of ice axes or double boots, let alone the hi-tech variety I climbed with. Without the luggage the expedition would be heading home, dreams of ascending anything quashed, long before even reaching the mountain. If the link to success was to be an enthusiastic viticulturist, we'd just have to go along.

The Hotel Nutibara's lights shimmered as if the power were low and the lift creaked from floor to floor. The beds were designed for economy size people to fit the equally condensed room. The air conditioner rattled and the shower was equipped with hotel-issue disinfectant soap. Somewhere in the city the luggage rested, hopefully at the airport. If not, this was going to be a very short trip to South America.

CHAPTER 5

BODEGA TO BASE CAMP

RAOUL ARRIVED EARLY, when thick white-bread toast lightly browned and grainy black coffee was still stacked on the breakfast table. 'I love America,' he said. 'It is businesslike, it is professional, it makes great wine. I spent a week with Robert Mondavi in California, working with him. He is a great man. You know his wine?' We rattled off in his Toyota. 'Oh yes,' he said, 'I've checked on your luggage, it's in the airline office. They said it is big and very heavy. They want it moved right now. We can pick it up now so you know it's safe and you and the airline will both be happy, *si*? Then we'll go to the *bodega*.' Just like that. Life was solved, the sun came out and Raoul was blessed. With the luggage stacked in heaps in the back, the South American breezes wafting off the vineyards and through the windows, the adventure could begin in earnest. A mountaineer without his ice axe is a very shaky character.

On my first visit to Argentina three years previously, I'd imagined Mendoza as a dusty village, like the town in the last stand of *Butch Cassidy and the Sundance Kid*, with the Andes jutting heavenward on the edge of town. Instead there were broad tree-lined avenues, Calvin Klein shops and outdoor restaurants set with endless rows of Spanish beauties whiling away their evenings sipping espressos. It was hard to imagine a more difficult city to leave.

'Mendoza is growing,' said Raoul. 'Nearly a million people now. The wine, you know, it gets better all the time.' Set in the heart of one of South America's largest wine-producing areas, Mendoza was like an oasis in the midst of Argentina's ups and downs.

'Here we are,' and the Toyota bounced through a large gate and into a courtyard. Boardwalks lined the terrraced whitewashed buildings, flowers sprung from the borders. Ferns hung from the dark wood rafters. The smell of fermenting wine and oak drifted on the air. Raoul was at home as he led us through mashers and mixers, vats and barrels, to their cellar. Long rows of French oak casks 10 metres round sat on their edge. 'America uses only stainless steel now,' Raoul said, 'but they are very expensive. Perhaps in a few years we will change.' The aroma of dark-stained oak permeated the building. The stainless steel may have been the winemaker's dream, but nothing could replace the veritable forest of natural dark wood set in the shadows of the oversized barn. Outside were rows of grapes and a rose garden, flowers hanging heavy and odorous in tunnelled walkways.

'Now, a small reward for our morning's work,' said Raoul as we returned to his office, set in the cool terrace of the entrance way. Bottles rescued from the cellar on the tour came out, glasses lined up, the vintages were poured. A glass of wine always tastes better when its history has been tracked. The luggage was safe and the introduction to South America had landed us in the heart of the wine country and it was only 11 a.m. We retreated to the hotel clutching several bottles for the onward journey. 'Don't forget to let me know how your climb goes,' said Raoul, waving farewells as he clanked his way back to work.

That afternoon I met with Archie, a raconteur who deals in antiques, the ambiguous field of 'import/export' and mules. Typical of people who get ahead in the more difficult circumstances found in less affluent countries, he was happy to deal in almost anything and knew how to short-circuit the details to get things done quickly. His business manner would frighten off anyone looking for a simple, straightforward arrangement such as is often found in the West. But because he operated outside the strict rules, his own reputation was important and results, once the deal was made, were guaranteed. Often people who operate beyond the normal business parameters are more trustworthy than those who rely on the back-up of lawyers and accountants. If what you are doing is illegal, you have to have a high level of trust with those you are doing business with. Our requirements were legal and relatively straightforward, but climbing permits, a van to the peak, accommodation and mules could be organised quickly or slowly and be expensive or otherwise. Avoiding *mañana* mentality was essential in Mendoza if any momentum was to be maintained.

'Four mules in and out from Base Camp on the Glacier, transport the 230 kilometres to Puenta del Inca, a night at the hotel, a permit. US$2,300, and the coffee is on me.' Archie liked the friendly touch; he was the king of added value, even if it was only a double espresso. 'Sure you don't need a cook, a señorita to cook, a chef really! And to clean, and,' he winked at me, 'to tuck you in at night. It can be very cold on Aconcagua you know.'

The deal was done, minus the Señorita, with departure set for dawn. The supermarket yielded up mixes, spices, and pasta, as well as anything that looked good in the pictures on the packaging, the answer to my rudimentary Spanish. In 1989, Paul Teare and I had run low on food on the South Face of Aconcagua and were left with only a small box of breakfast cereal to see us through the final two days, praising its restorative qualities. On our return we realised that what we thought was high energy breakfast cereal had actually been concentrated baby food.

Joe and I settled into an early evening meal at a sidewalk café. Joe's voluminous and flashy camera equipment attracted the attention of the waiters, and Joe, in his friendly enthusiasm to show off, was happy to oblige them.

'It's gone! Robert, it's gone, my camera bag's gone!'

I'd been rereading the menu, trying to remember the basics of Spanish food.

'My passport was in there!' Joe grabbed a waiter. They spoke no English and only nodded their heads sadly. Joe rushed off up the street. The disappearance had happened so quickly that retrieving anything was impossible; it bore the mark of professionals who would have disappeared into the myriad of back alleys immediately. A pizza and a beer assisted my contemplation of our next move.

'What are we going to do?' Joe returned, distraught. Speaking no Spanish, he had quickly become frustrated in his search. 'Talk to Archie,' I suggested. 'I'll phone him after dinner.'

'Don't worry,' said Archie when I rang, immediately in his element. 'It's happened to my friends before. You don't need a passport to travel in Argentina anyway and the only place you can replace it is at the American Embassy in Buenos Aires. We'll go around to the police station tomorrow morning and get a temporary pass, you'll be out of town early afternoon. I'll see you at breakfast at nine, the police don't get up too early.'

Joe felt naked without his passport and even worse for losing it. 'I've lived in New York for years. I should know better.' I had to agree. As the mountain loomed, patience levels were growing shorter. The luggage had been twelve hours of nerves, now we were minus a passport and with the added weight of feeling incompetent twice over. How was I going to get around the world and back after a start like this?

Behind the counter of the police station, sitting upright on a tall stool, a small ceramic statue of the Virgin Mary looking down on her from the wall above, was the policewoman. Her crisp blue uniform was perfectly pressed, her hair pulled back with tendrils framing her neck, her gun nestled confidently against her hip. I forgot my Spanish lessons. Luckily, Archie was in tow; a free service, he assured me, looking after his clients. 'Besides,' he encouraged me, 'Argentina is not like it used to be. Don't be afraid.' I could only agree, as the policewoman stared at us with her big brown eyes. Joe filled out forms and more forms. At noon we escaped, travel permit in hand. With the mandatory steak sandwich under our belts and the van loaded, we headed west.

The Andes are the longest mountain range in the world, containing the tallest peaks outside of the Himalayas. Following an Everest expedition in 1988, I'd travelled south, looking for something high and hard to climb. The South Face Direct on Aconcagua had a frightening reputation, so I brought Paul Teare, who'd been on Everest, with me. Paul is rarely frightened, as well as being a master at hard mixed climbing, when the ice is rotten, thin and melting, and the rock steep and broken. This ensured we made the summit four and a half days after we started. We'd travelled this same road together and experienced the hardest face on Aconcagua already, providing added inspiration for a return to the second highest of the Seven Summits for a solo attempt. I'd be climbing a completely different route, but the approach and the mood of the mountain was known, its storms, rock and ice familiar, the most important aspect of climbing any peak.

The road wove out of Mendoza, through the vineyards, past a refinery spitting fire and into the dry lowlands of the Andean foothills. The highway, a major transport route from Argentina over the Andes, eventually dropped over into Santiago, Chile, on the far side of the mountains. Hot, dry air filtered in the windows as the van roared over the flats and into a deep river valley. The hills rose up thousands of metres overhead, but they were mere toddlers, oversized hillocks protecting the main range. As ever when entering the mountains, they looked so big; too big. The stereo played the Argentinian Top 40. Afternoon tea was another steak sandwich. Steaks are eaten at all meals. Breakfast steak, lunch steak, and the choice of pepper, garlic, onion or mushroom steak for dinner. Vegetarians quickly perish in Argentina.

The air turned from the thick, hot wavy heat of the plains to the thin clear air of the mountains as the hills squeezed in close to the road. The river formed rapids and the rolling nature of the hills changed abruptly to cliffs, rocks rising over the road with bands of colour slicing in arcs of brown and orange like rainbows cutting through them. The engine ground along as the air thinned, slowing as the rise to the pass loomed. The road markers at the side of the road grew to 3 metres high, the tops orange-tipped to direct the snowploughs in winter. A ski area loomed beside the road, grey granite lodge and wooden-peaked roofs, Swiss style — why does every ski lodge copy the Swiss? Half an hour away was the low-slung hotel of Puenta del Inca, set at the apex of the pass into Chile. The seven bags were dumped on the ground, a four-bed dormitory room booked, two beds for us, two for the bags. Thin mattresses on wooden slats covered with even thinner blankets and blazing red covers lent a warm homely air to the room. The window opened out onto a bare hill stretching heavenward. In an environment of peaks edging 7,000 metres, the hills stretched to over 5,000, but barely warranted a second glance.

'Knock, knock, *mulas*?' I'd met Ricardo three years before, after he'd rescued our 'lost' equipment from some less than scrupulous gauchos who'd 'found' it and brought it down the mountain, yet failed to find who it belonged to. He dragged our bags off to be weighed and sent up the mountain. We'd see the bags every night, but during the day the mules would gallop up the hills with them, ensuring us of fresh vegetables, fried eggs for breakfast and even a celebratory bottle of red wine from our friendly winery.

The air felt thin and cold already, the unheated room and open window a constant reminder of the mountain's closeness. The last refuge, the hot shower, ran cold at dawn the next morning, changing the last comfort of civilisation into a thirty-second soap and dash for the towel. Ricardo drove us back down the road to the trail head, an innocuous valley extending for kilometres uphill and around corners with no peak in sight. He waved good-bye and drove off, leaving us in a cloud of dust. I shouldered my pack. 'Every journey starts with the first step, every climb starts with the first move,' echoed inanely in my head. First steps were unsteady, the pack an alien being clutching my back, full of needless weight. Why hadn't I given more to the mules, what did I need a spare pair of shoes for? Were two litres of water really necessary when walking next to a river? The map had detailed a wander up a valley for 15 or 20 kilometres, following a rough trail. I'd left a desk job for this? The morning dragged, the heat turned sinister and pants were exchanged for shorts, sun lotion, a hat. It was like a long walk on a rocky beach. The mountains were nowhere to be seen, surrounded by brown, dry hills covered in low brush and small cliffs. The trail was indistinct and split into hydra-headed paths leading nowhere that had to be retraced.

A huge swath of snow lurked in the shadows, an avalanche from high above that had swept down and bridged the river. A tunnel of ice melted out below and the river disappeared into the dark cave. The trail led up to the edge and onto the ice, then a light trail led over the bridge, scuffed into the dirt covering the ice. The bridge was 20 metres across, the river 10 metres below. It looked solid, but it was obviously due to cave in sometime soon, maybe as I crept over it? Maybe not? I scuttled across, watching the rapids curl away below, imagining the plunge through the ice into the depths, the pack dragging me over, bouncing off the rocks. I had no mountain sense yet, no confidence. But the bridge cut me off from the comforts below. As I slid gratefully back onto solid earth on the other side of the torrent, some of the apprehension and the feeling of remorse at leaving civilisation faded away. Fear had sent the adrenalin through me, cleansing the city from the pores.

Lunch was a steak sandwich packed by the hotel, with a side of boiled eggs and fried bread. A belief in high-protein, high-fat cooking is firmly entrenched in the Argentinian culture, a diet that the only answer to is a siesta. Awaking, I found rain splattering my face, cold, straight out of the clouds bred in the high mountains. The mules toiled up the trail below, their hooves kicking up small dust storms. They reached us quickly and trotted past, heads low, sides heaving, the gaucho on their tail waving an enormous whip, popping it between their floppy ears when they strayed. 'Una hora, una hora,' he waved ahead and laughed. One hour could mean anything to a man with no watch and a herd of galloping mules. Sunrise and sunset was relevant, but anything in between was very fluid to people who lived in the hills. Two hours passed as the hill went on and on, then a plume of smoke puffed over the rise ahead as the rain returned with a vengeance. Camp was a big boulder and a stone cabin, already occupied by the gauchos huddled in the doorway, laughing at us as we clambered down the hill dripping wet and unrolled the flapping tent.

The eight-man tepee was extravagant but eminently comfortable, a shelter large enough to stand up in, toss all the packs into and still create an inside kitchen on an oversized rock. Pat Smith, an enthusiastic outdoor equipment designer and founder of Mountainsmith in Colorado, had given it to me a month earlier. 'Just try it out. It's more like a cabin than a tent.' The first night out convinced me. The tent was close to having everything but the kitchen sink. As my climbing partner from New York, Steve Sanford, with whom I'd ascended Ball's Pyramid, had commented, 'Let's be as comfortable as possible as long as possible — then we can suffer.' In the morning, I rolled out of my sleeping bag, stood up and got dressed. It wasn't quite home, but over the next year, the tepee would be the next best thing.

'Hola, hola,' or something like it echoed from the gauchos at dawn. Ricardo had warned us about the river crossing. 'I have asked the gauchos to take you across. Make sure and get up early or they will leave you to cross on your own.'

The river was a 15-metre wide swath filled with frothing waves tossed up by submerged boulders. Stories of climbers knocked over and dragged downstream for kilometres before they crawled out battered and bruised, forced to retreat before they even reached Aconcagua, were common. Having overcome lost luggage and stolen passports, the last thing we needed was to drown in the river. With the rain still pouring down, the pack packed and the mule bags carefully stuffed with a few extras there was no reason to carry, we made the quick walk to the river. The gaucho laughed and slapped the back of his saddle. The mule was a cross between a New Zealand racehorse and a giraffe. I threw my foot into the loose stirrup and slid in behind the gaucho, the mule hot-footing in circles until the whip flew past my nose onto the animal's flank. The mule straightened out and headed into the water. The water rose up under its belly as it dropped into holes and the torrent rushed up my legs. The mule staggered, lurched upstream, looked over its shoulder as if it wanted to turn around, the whip flew past again and it lunged up the bank, my arms wrapped around the gaucho's waist. The mule trotted onto flat ground and I slid off the back with relief. What a way to wake up. No orange juice, no coffee, soaked feet and another 15 kilometres to walk up the rocky trail to the next camp.

The trail wove along the river, over washes and into the dry river bed. In the early afternoon three figures appeared as dots ahead, looking like Lawrence of Arabia coming out of the desert. 'Hi, I'm Skip Horner.' I introduced myself. 'We were lucky,' he added, 'the weather was good for just a couple days. We still didn't make the Polish Glacier, had to go around to the Normal Route. Lots of people have tried the Glacier, but no one's been up there in quite a while. A bit harder than most people think. And it's a lot easier to go around the corner.' He spoke with the authority of a guide, who with his two paying clients in tow, had to resort to the easier route. They all had the rough austerity that several weeks of living in the mountains and reaching the summit gives people. It started to rain and, as they set off downhill in a rush, I cautiously dug out my raincoat. I wanted to be brave and hardy, but the city ways still trailed after me, the uncertainty that only a few weeks in the mountains and on the summit could wash away.

The valley opened out and the gauchos' stone hut appeared on a hill above the river. To the west, the sun cut through the chasm that led to Base Camp. Aconcagua suddenly appeared from around the corner. The peak rose in a symmetrical pyramid, a cascading flow of white icefalls and rocky cliffs building to a pinpoint summit. Still 15 kilometres distant, clouds wreathed the top, then cleared, while closer, snow fell on the glaciers. A final bank of cloud had built up overhead for the afternoon rainstorm. One mountain and three weather systems existed between our camp and the summit.

Having run down the Normal Route after ascending the South Face, I'd thought this side may have been the same, a route of slaggy terraces and uninspiring slopes with no view of the top. But the Polish Glacier swept down off the summit ridge and onto the glacier in a long sunlit slope of ice. It was steep and inviting. I'd not wanted to ascend the vertical mud cliffs and rotting ice of the South Face again, but neither had I wanted the terminal physical boredom of the Normal Route. This looked impressive, yet not so difficult it couldn't be soloed quickly. The mountain wrapped itself up in darkness and faded through the door of the tepee as the potatoes boiled merrily on the stove. Finally, there was a mountain to look at.

The tent was on clean white sand, a bank along the river built up in the high spring rains. It was a flat, embracing bed without the stones and puddles of the previous night. Occasionally, safe in a civilised bed and thinking about an upcoming adventure, I'd be frightened with the thought of being so close to the earth. But when I actually arrived in the mountains, sleeping on the ground was more comfortable and more secure than being at home. By morning the rains had extended the river into 10-metre-wide rivulets a metre or so deep, not nearly the deadly torrent of the previous day. Since we had been chatting to the gauchos for the past two days, sharing food and giving them small presents of ropes, matches and cigarettes, they waited at the river bank for us. The mules didn't even seem to notice our weight as they galloped through the water, fresh from their night's sleep.

Three years previously I'd descended from the top of Aconcagua exhausted and out of food after completing the South Face. At the base of the normal route at Plaza de Mulas, the highest place the mules are allowed, there is still a 40-kilometre walk out down a rock-strewn gulch. Wearing stiff plastic double boots down the rocky trail wasn't a pleasant thought. Having spent my youth in Western Colorado, I fancied myself a natural rider. So twenty dollars and some arm-waving later I'd negotiated a ride on a small, black and very stocky female mule.

The mule trot was teeth-chattering, the saddle was crossed with wooden T-bars for carrying duffle bags, covered with a rapidly punctured Therm-a-rest air pad. Three hours into the ride, the gaucho having insisted on leading her down the hill with the oversized gringo in the saddle, little Blacky spooked, reared up and dumped me on my backside in a pile of rocks. I retrieved the reins from the gaucho and rode Blacky in circles, away from the gaucho's looming whip. He had suddenly seen any tip he may have imagined flying away as fast as I'd flown through the air and was going to beat Blacky into her proper subservient role. Blacky soon realised I was the lesser of two evils and acquiesced to the reins and a bit of gentle prodding. The gaucho was happy for me to wander down the hill at a more sedate pace, taking turns to walk when the T-bars felt like they were going to cut my skinny body in half. At the end of the day I slid off Blacky and collapsed to my knees, not sure whether the walk would have been worse than the ride, but with a healthy respect for the toughness of the mountain mules.

After crossing the river the trail led up a narrow defile cut by a tumbling stream. Guanaco footprints were everywhere, but the real thing hid just out of sight around the next corner of the twisting trail. With the trail an easy strip of red sand bordered by alpine bushes, the peak rose like the Matterhorn of the Andes at the head of the valley. Scudding clouds cast shadows over the kilometres of glacier as they stretched down off the summit ridge and wound around the rock towers into the valley below. The mountain gained form and the route to the summit stood out. It wound into a series of rock towers set like skyscrapers at 5,500 metres, then out onto the skyline, traversing the very edge of a 1,000-metre cliff before tackling the final icefall for which the route was named, the Polish Glacier. A final 700-metre walk, with one foot on the East Face and another on the South Face, led directly to the summit. The afternoon clouds rolled around the summit, forming dark grey bands with tendrils floating off them. Weather at 4,000 metres was nothing like it would be 3,000 metres higher at the top.

CHAPTER 6

THE WANDERING GUANACO

BASE CAMP. ROCKS, big and little. Red rocks, orange rocks, yellow rocks. Rocks everywhere. Tiny platforms built by climbers who had gone before, climbers who had succeeded and climbers who had failed. No one had hollowed out enough ground for an eight-man tepee so we set to work, enlarging an enclave, building the walls up and flattening the floor. The wind blew in gusts, blasts from the nearby glacier filled with ice. Ten people occupied Base Camp, spread around in tiny mountain tents, occasionally surfacing to run down the hill for water or to look up the hill at the gathering clouds.

A lanky bearded Argentinian wandered over and formally introduced himself as the ranger for the camp. 'Name of Guillermo,' he informed me, smiling brightly. His only link with civilisation was through a fickle radio, the antenna strung out between a series of rocks next to Base Camp. His duties were rescues and garbage. Rescues were infrequent, usually involving little more than dialling a helicopter, collecting $2,000 and sending the injured party off into the sky. He passed me a garbage bag and explained its obvious use. Even my Spanish understood this. It was soon evident he was very bored, helping to pitch our tent, taking me to get water, filling me in on camp gossip: who'd summited, who hadn't, who slept with who in the tents, who's *señorita* was the most vocal, demonstrated by graphic hip movements and tipping his head back and howling. Sex was never far from the South American male's thoughts, yet it was all done with a familiar earthiness that was more good-natured than disrespectful, directing as much humour at themselves as at their partners. The Spanish dictionary found a permanent place in my pocket, to get through the more complex subjects Guillermo wanted to discuss, as he frequently seemed to pop up from behind one rock or another, eager for a conversation.

The night was restless, gusts buffeting the big tent, the thin air failing to refuel the body. The tepee was a welcome home in the morning, the stove torched into action from the warmth of the sleeping bag, while other climbers outside cursed the wind as they huddled in the lee of a rock or breathed gas fumes in the alcoves of their tents. Altitude dictated a rest day for physical reasons, while mentally I needed a rest from the walk in. Once I actually got to the climbing I always felt fine, but the basic walking required to reach the big mountains always seemed far harder than it should be. The 'three day walk-in to Base Camp' that rolled off the tongue in planning for the climb had proved exhausting. But the mules had done their job well and not a single egg had been broken, so we had the basis for an immediate breakfast, followed by a nap until lunch. Then the weather deteriorated and there was no reason to leave the tent at all. Climbing mountains dictated periods of hyperactivity balanced with periods of complete collapse. The best way to acclimatise was to sleep, eat and drink. Movement only slowed things down, so living sloth-like was the ideal way to acclimatise quickly.

The pre-expedition food shop had yielded up everything from garlic the size of lemons to spicy Italian sausages. Anything that resembled freeze-dried or pre-packaged food had been avoided. The Argentinian supermarket had ensured a food supply that would have made an Italian restaurant proud; it included our very small but well-aged wine cellar, compliments of Raoul. On my first overseas excursion years before, living and working for six months in Norway, I'd met a group of Norwegian climbers who spent most weekends climbing. Being part of a new young breed of alpinist, they had spurned the traditional Norwegian Alpine Club, with its articles of conduct founded on rules written by ancient trolls. In defiance, they'd formed the 'Norwegian Alpine Dining Club' whose motto, 'the ability to take the lead on the most difficult climbs and in the most difficult menus', spurred them to prepare culinary extravaganzas in all storms and against all odds. The ability to prepare a seven-course meal on a one-burner primus stove — a different wine with every course, a liberal lacing of akavit, the Norwegian national liquor, and Cuban cigars wafting into the star-studded nights along the fjords — was a minimal requirement for entrance.

If cooking the meal was one small feat, getting up the long and difficult routes lining Norway's fjords with all the trimmings in the pack was another. Little wonder the Norwegian Alpine Dining Club's reputation soon took on mythical proportions. The President, Lars Stendahl, a man who became a good friend and with whom I was to later climb the Northwest Face of Half Dome in Yosemite, California, introduced me to club values early on in my career. When I attempted to skip a course of 'cloud berries in cream' with the excuse I was getting 'full', he said, 'At the Norwegian Alpine Dining Club, we don't eat and drink until we are full, we eat and drink until we are sick.' Luckily, in the land of the midnight sun, where climbing could start at dawn, dinner was often interrupted by breakfast with a return to the rocks shortly thereafter.

The Norwegian Alpine Dining Club belief, that food quality should not be sacrificed just because you are in the mountains, continued to rule all menu plans. With bags of fresh food, seven different types of pasta, a box of white baby potatoes, tiny hot red and green chillies, capsicum, spring onions, a can of Greek olives, two litres of olive oil and a rather large pepper grinder, the mule loads had been worth every kilo. There was also a large row of sausages hanging outside Guillermo's tent indicating there would be some support if supplies ran low. For all this fine food, it soon became apparent I'd followed my dictum on fresh food so strongly there was virtually no snack or easily eaten trail food like chocolate or crackers. The result was bowls of potato soup packed in thermos flasks for lunch, laced with grated parmesan cheese and a slice of peperoni on top. Joe diplomatically smiled but never complained.

The Polish Route on Aconcagua has its Base Camp at just over 4,000 metres, Camp I at 4,800, Camp II at 5,800, Camp III at 6,200 and the summit at 6,960 metres. In the previous two weeks, seven groups had failed to get up the Polish Glacier. They had either turned back entirely or taken a traverse from Camp II in a long loop around the mountain to the north side and then ascended the Normal Route. Having descended the Normal Route in 1989 after ascending the South Face, I had no desire to go anywhere near it. Used by anyone who simply wants to get to the top, it has become little more than a steep trail to the summit. If it were less used it might be somewhat interesting as it winds its long but circuitous way up to the top. But the hordes of people, trash floating in the wind, tin cans clanking under foot, latrines, toilet paper, dead mules and even the occasional frozen body alongside the trail make it perhaps the least pleasant route to the top of any of the Seven Summits.

As I looked through binoculars at the Polish Glacier from Base Camp, the avalanche troughs that crossed the route stood out. Every afternoon, wind and snow storms blew in, leaving snowfall of 2–3 centimetres low down, which translated to ten or more centimetres up high. With no chance to consolidate, the glacier was continuously dangerous, ready to cut loose in an avalanche and bury me at any time.

The following morning, with a load of food and a tent in the packs, we set off up the hill to Camp I. Climbing at altitude requires several weeks to acclimatise, best undertaken by climbing high and returning to camp to sleep before moving up the mountain. An indistinct trail wound up the hill outside of camp before crossing onto the glacier, where we were treading on loose rocks set into the ice. Base Camp disappeared from sight quickly and the English Glacier rolled down from the heights to the left, tumbling in long icefalls to crash into a hidden valley far overhead. Its tail reached out across the path, the distinctive Andean Penitente rising for tens of metres off the glacier.

The temperature extremes in the Andes form these huge, thin

ice towers in the glaciers called Penitentes, the wind cutting them into the fantastic shapes of geometrically formed monsters. In the morning sun, water dripped off their edges and the soft snow sucked at our feet as we wove through the maze. Inside the Penitentes, avenues ran between the ice towers, like secret passageways lined with guards. Tunnels were threaded and crevasses skirted before we popped back onto solid ground on the far side. A final hill, skirting the side of the glacier, led to a small terrace, covered in alpine grass, already dusted white with the afternoon snowstorm. We dropped the tent and a bag of food and headed back to Base Camp.

The weather held at consistently bad. 'More snow than sun, more wind than fun,' I recited as we took another day off. Above camp, a bare hill with a view over the glacier and into the lower valleys provided ideal guanaco-watching potential. Their trails were evident on the far hillsides, their lives dictated by grazing and romping over the hills and down to the river for a drink in the evenings. But they remained ever elusive, always just out of sight.

The following day, with packs stacked high overhead with provisions, including the small sack of potatoes, and feeling distinctly like mules, we staggered up the well-known trail and settled into the tiny tent at Camp I. In residence were five climbers from the American Alpine Club, moving equipment from Camp I to Camp II. 'More snow than should be here at this time of year,' said one, pointing up the hill. 'When we got here this entire hill was bare to the rock. Now it practically looks like a glacier.'

I tried not to get depressed, hoping for a break in the weather for a day or two. I set off alone early the following morning with a day pack to see what the route ahead looked like. Three and a half hours later I wandered into Camp II at 5,800 metres. Camp II was set amongst a city of rock towers, huge yellow-orange pillars towering 20 metres high, surrounded by ice and small stones. It was a spectacular, if windy and heartless, place. A few tents set at crazy angles sheltered in the lee of the rocks, which provided little protection from the wind. Disjointed conversation came from inside one tent. 'Is that somebody, I thought I heard somebody,' as I wandered past. 'Get the stove going then will you, I did it last time and my feet are cold, where's the pee bottle?' whined out into the wind as I headed out to the base of the Polish Glacier. The AAC climbers had said some people had been in Camp II for five days waiting for the weather to clear. Five days at 5,800 metres in a perpetual storm would make anybody whine.

The glacier wasn't much of a traditional glacier in its upper reaches, falling 700 metres from the ridge to Camp II at an average angle of 45 degrees. Avalanche trails swept down the left and right sides of the glacier. Getting anywhere near the traditional route up the left side would be very dangerous, even though it provided the easiest ascent. However, through the centre was a line of terraces and ramps that led directly towards the ridge. It didn't look entirely stable, but climbing solo I wouldn't be waiting around and could ascend the most dangerous areas without stopping.

What the route made more dangerous through snowfall would be compensated for by choosing a direct line broken by the steepest part of the icefall and then climbing quickly through it. I put the binoculars back in the pack and started down. Just above Camp II I saw the body resting in the snow, partially covered with drifts. It looked like little more than a collapsed tent, a cloth skeleton. At this altitude it would take a monumental effort to drag it down the hill and no one came here to drag bodies around, so there it stayed. It seemed as good a grave as any. The face was pinched tight, a tiny smile on the lips, eyes closed. Strangely, it didn't seem out of place in the harsh environment, just someone who had become too tired and lain down to rest for too long. I suppose it is still there.

CHAPTER 7

SOUTH AMERICAN SUMMITS

THE PREVIOUS DAY'S snowstorm melted by mid-morning and the sun was warm and welcoming, an omen that good weather really did exist, if only in patches. Below camp, the glacier dropped off steeply in a roll and then popped out again next to Base Camp before sliding off into the valley below. The cliffs that had towered over Base Camp now swept up immediately across from Camp I. The sun never touched their southern exposure and icicles close to 1,000 metres long dripped off them. By early afternoon the heat would loosen a tendril or two off the main mass of ice and they would shatter, peeling over the rock and tumbling into the rocks below. Camp I rested in a narrow gorge, opening out behind into the route up the mountain, a shallow V leading to a ridge and on up to Camp II, just visible on the horizon. Camp I was a tiny oasis where a few plumes of alpine grass sprouted and a tiny afternoon stream trickled down beside the tent, formed from melting snow.

That afternoon, three Austrian climbers staggered down the hill and into Camp I. 'Robert, you should have a look at this guy's feet,' Joe called over. Having lost a toe and a half to frostbite, I'd learned everything I could about prevention to avoid a repeat experience. For what I originally believed to be a simple ailment, I soon discovered as many different treatments as toes left on my feet. First-aid kit in hand, I went over to where the Austrian rested against a rock, his feet propped up in the sand. I stifled a gasp at the first glance at his toes. Every toe was solid black in colour and swollen to twice normal size all the way back to where they joined his foot.

Underneath, the frozen blackness extended up into the pads of the balls of his feet. It was obvious that he would, at the least, lose his toes. The toes were already mushy and dead, blisters beginning to form around his foot, popping out in purple and black bubbles. While I cleaned them up as best I could the Austrian climber related his story.

Trapped by bad weather for several days at Camp II, they'd finally had a chance to go for the summit. The deep snow had hindered climbing and he'd started with wet boots. Climbing all through the day in deep snow, they'd traversed across to the Normal Route and followed that to the summit, descending late in the day into darkness. A tiny hut filled with ice provided them with little shelter and without sleeping bags or tent they'd huddled together through the night at 6,400 metres, before creeping out at dawn across the long traverse back to their supplies at Camp II.

Packing up quickly they'd retreated down the mountain to Camp I. He had not had his boots off in the last three days and though suspecting his toes were getting cold and numb, hadn't felt they were all ready to drop off. I gave him some aspirin and Adalat to aid circulation and since he was a few days and a long walk from civilisation, antibiotics to help stop any infection. 'You should ride a mule out,' I encouraged, but he shook his head and said in a thick Austrian accent, 'I do not like those animals, I walk.' He was a scientific doctor in Austria, obviously highly intelligent and an experienced mountaineer, who had made the one mistake of climbing higher with cold feet. I tried to encourage him as best I could, knowing frostbite often looks far worse than it turns out. But with toes black and mushy three days from the road, I couldn't see them having much chance to improve. He tottered off down the hill full of tea and best wishes. I wandered back to our tent, the stove bubbling merrily away in happy contrast to the black, festering toes that hovered in front of my eyes.

Before I'd set off for Aconcagua I'd had a rough plan of starting from as low as possible on the mountain, climbing quickly to the summit and returning to camp in a day. What actually constitutes a solo isn't well defined so I established my own criteria. I felt I should climb alone and unassisted from where the mountain really began, where the hard climbing started. The Polish Glacier didn't start until after Camp II, anything before that being little more than a hike between camps. Base Camp was the highest mule transport but didn't define the start of the mountain, any more than our three-day walk from the road-head had. I knew that where the climb started would be different on each of the Seven Summits and soloing them was an arbitrary definition.

At one point in my planning I'd got out a world map and figured out how long and hard it would be to go from sea level on each continent to the summit under my own power, utilising bicycle and foot travel. But the logistics and costs seemed more trouble than it was worth. I decided I was a climber and I'd stick to the climbing. As many of the peaks had relatively easy routes to the top, I'd choose more difficult ascents whenever practical, climbing them as fast as possible. I'd not use ropes or fix any protection, relying only on ice axe and crampons. Having soloed vertical rock climbs since I was 15, I trusted my climbing instincts to carry me through the more difficult peaks. To summarise, when the 'climbing' started, I'd go solo. If the peak didn't have any really difficult ground, I'd start where the peak seemed to start. While in theory this wasn't well defined, each of the Seven Summits turned out to have a natural start point, so in the end it was easy to decide where to start my 'solos' from.

On Aconcagua, the mountain really started at Camp II. But the distance from Camp I to Camp II wasn't great so I thought perhaps starting from Camp I and ascending the entire 2,160 metres from there to the summit in one push might be possible. The ascent would have to be done quickly with no delays, even in the steeper sections, and the deep snow would have to turn to ice higher up to make climbing faster. And hopefully I'd be fit enough to stay on my feet that long, after being at altitude for little more than a week. As long as I kept just a little in reserve to get down, I could turn around at any point.

I could afford to fail and try again. Inside, I knew this was the last thing I wanted to do. But the rationale allowed me to carry on with the plan. I told Joe my idea, but cautioned him to mention it to no one. With groups piling off the mountain with altitude sickness and frostbite, and mumbling about the terrible conditions, I didn't care to discuss my notion of literally running out of one of the lower camps, dashing to the summit and back in a day. Other groups struggled to get from Camp I to the summit in five days and a number became stuck for weeks, so I didn't want to appear to be belittling their efforts.

One of the most enjoyable aspects of climbing is the lack of formal rules and the opportunity to attempt the biggest and hardest peaks in whatever style one wishes. It is like being able to compete immediately in the Olympics or challenge for the heavyweight championship of the world, depending entirely on one's own resources. The single big difference with high altitude alpinism is that a mistake doesn't just mean you lose. It can leave you with shorter feet, or worse, frozen permanently in place. Aconcagua had never been shy in reminding climbers of that.

Sleep was filled with black toes, avalanches and visions of endless ice-fields. At midnight the alarm sounded, a space-age beep piercing the night. Getting up at midnight for a projected 2 a.m. start could hardly be a night's sleep. The weakened high altitude mind struggled with the logic of it, a low-level headache resulted and the stove fumes gassed the brain. Half asleep, I didn't let doubt or thoughts of why I was doing this intrude. The basics — the stove going, the coffee and chocolate sipped, the muesli eaten, the hot water bottles filled — propelled the morning. Then the clothes were slid into, frost falling off against the skin. Finally and always least pleasant, the boots were pulled from under my head, the two pairs of socks pulled on, stretched to allow no wrinkles or constrictions, remembering the black Austrian toes for a second, the laces set loosely around the inner boots, the plastic outer boot wrapped over the top and strapped down and finally the super gaiters pulled down tight over the welt and velcroed into place.

Feeling half asleep, I unfolded from the tent, the sky black and star-studded. The pack already waited, the hot water bottles slid down the sides, the straps pulled tight.

At 2.30 a.m. I finally waved goodbye to Joe and set off up the hill. It was pitch black and had snowed again late the previous day, so tracks leading uphill had faded. An hour later a steep cliff rose up and I realised I'd crossed the gorge and bumped into the far wall, having completely missed the way. I fell into waist-deep holes between boulders as a reverse led back towards the middle of the gorge. I had wanted to shoot straight out of camp and now I was wandering around in a morass of snow, headlamp picking out unknown shadows and shapes. Upwards, just keep going upwards. Stopping for a second would only precipitate a return to the tent. But I had studied the weather very closely and this looked to be the one good day in a long stormy season. The weather pattern seemed to be snow for three to five days then, without warning, clear skies for a day, then snow again. Higher winds the day before appeared to have blown the storm away and waiting another day would make it too late. At 4 a.m. there were no clouds and a steady wind, all of which I interpreted as good signs. The groups who'd been failing in droves were all looking for many days in a row to make their summit push. I needed only one day. One perfect day.

Stomp, stomp. There is little inspiration in snow slogging, but it did get me back into the gulch, the stars leading me upwards. The route grew steeper up to the ridge, turned left, and then the mass of Aconcagua stood out ahead. No moon, a star-filled night, the horizon tinged with the very faintest of light only a shade above pitch black, as though there was a bucket of stars hiding over the eastern horizon. Up, up, up. The towers of Camp II loomed.

The horizon tinged with orange as I crept through Camp II, tents ghostly and sleeping in the pre-dawn dark. It was icy cold, the wind cutting across the ridge, frozen into icy blasts in the 5,800 metre air. I stopped and set up the video camera for a dawn interview with myself, freezing solid in the process, the two-hour battery draining away in ten minutes. So much for technology. At least now I could concentrate on the climbing.

The sun burst over the horizon as the route started up the glacier. The ice above glowed ominously orange in the sunrise. The altitude was already slowing the pace, allowing plenty of time to eye the ramps and terraces leading up the icefall. To the left, the traditional Polish Glacier route swept up an easy ramp, a hundred metres of ice that led to the ridge where some parties paused for a night at Camp III. Even in the half light the snow hugging the upper slopes was clearly unstable, ready to release when the sun touched it, or with a step from the ice onto the snow. I curved into the centre of the face, ice jumbles, crevasses and all. It looked broken but stable, while I reassured myself I'd be rushing through it. The second ice axe came out in defence and I checked the bindings on the crampons, the blue ice underneath crisply taking the points without a quiver.

The icefall rolled overhead in a series of waves. The route led right beneath one tower, and up, left beneath another and up. But luck didn't last; the last two waves bulged out in icy monoliths, crevasses falling away below. The sun bored into the slope. Below, the ice swept down into the rock towers of Camp II, already a dot underfoot. The glacier rolled away and down past Camp II, Camp I, and then out to Base Camp. The view extended over the far ranges, into the red of the plains, the imagination leading on to the wineries and the fields stretching to the South Atlantic. Back on the ice I was tiny, minute.

The points of the ice tool set into the ice above led up a ramp, a sidewalk, then a curb, then a crack in the ice, crampons following, leveraged into the crack, ice tools pulling me up the bulging ice overhead. The ice became steeper as confidence grew, the ice world now dictating every move. Three more terraces followed, vertical humps, one a false start hiding only a mammoth crevasse just past the lip. A quick retreat, the crampons scrabbling for purchase as back-pedalling led down to a sloping ledge to catch my breath. A final icy corner loomed, ten metres, twenty metres, more than I wanted to contemplate climbing down at any altitude. Then I suddenly pulled over the rim and the icefield was below, 300 metres of jumbled ice tumbling off into the glacier. A final huge crevasse loomed, spanned only by a thin bridge crossed with a rush and a prayer. It had looked solid, or so I convinced myself on the far side.

It was 10 a.m. Four hours to get up the ice fall. But it was by far the hardest climbing of the route. Now I just had to keep going. By noon, the route led up to the ridge, with a 3,000-metre drop down the South Face on the other side. I traced the route I'd completed three years previously; the endless tiers of rock and ice, like five Polish Glaciers stacked one on top of the other, rolled away into the valley. Crystal-blue pools stood out in the valley like Cyclops' eyes, azure pools staring up from black rock-covered ice. The ridge was level with the summit ice-field where the two American alpinists had perished years before. Being close to the top of Aconcagua meant only one thing — it was further away from the safety of the lowlands.

The route led up the very apex of the ridge, a few kilometres of air on both sides of the crampons. There was over 500 metres of climbing to go, but gaining the ridge I'd rejoined the route taken by most climbers ascending the Polish Glacier and knew the way ahead couldn't be too difficult. The ridge was an unexpected pleasure now the glacier was below, a walk into heaven, arching up through breaths of cloud, crampons biting crisply into the ice. Two hours later enthusiasm turned to despair as the ridge went on and on. Breathing was rapid and laboured. Two thousand metres above Camp I in 12 hours was too much to ask. The ice axe became a cane as I struggled forward. Three p.m. Four p.m. The mind wandered off on its own. Maybe the peak didn't have a summit? Maybe I would be out here climbing forever into the clouds? The clouds faded and the afternoon sun returned, for the first time in weeks. I'd been blessed with good weather, my forecast having been marginally scientific and supremely lucky. Five p.m. The struggle was getting ugly, feet sloughed through the snow, tripping over rocks. Finally, over a snow slope the size of a football field and a final rock heap the silver cross at the summit glistened in the evening sun. A half hour later I took the final, faltering steps to the summit of Aconcagua.

Fifteen hours and 2,160 metres out of bed, I was finally at the top. The sun was sliding into the horizon, the wind stopped. It was weirdly warm, almost tropical for a peak just short of 7,000 metres in the sky. I sat down for a late lunch, a lukewarm cup of tea, a chocolate bar. Argentina rolled redly out to the east and Chile dropped rapidly off into the South Pacific to the west. The ridges of Aconcagua extended out into the bluest of skies, set off by the red earth holding the sky up on the horizon. Lunch revived me and photos in all directions spun out a circle view of the top of South America. The continent stretched out below with the Andes as its backbone, the longest mountain range on earth. A thousand kilometres north was 6,500-metre Huascaren, the first tall peak I'd soloed, back in 1981. Further north the range swept through Ecuador and into Colombia.

South the mountains stretched the length of Chile to Cape Horn, disappearing into the Southern Ocean. The white-peaked tops looked frosted, set against the red-orange rock, extending out into the deep brown hues of the plains. The summit seemed as close to the sky above as the earth below appeared from the top of the continent. The sun burned towards the Pacific Ocean, an orange orb diving towards the horizon beneath it. The shadows already reached out across Aconcagua's glaciers, rushing across the peak towards darkness. I hoisted my pack back to my shoulders, sheathed my ice axe and started the lonely journey back to Camp I.

After 15 hours spent reaching the summit, the ice and snow environment was second nature, crampons dancing down the ridge and out into the icefall. As darkness raced down the ice, a traverse dropped me into the avalanche chute leading down the far east side of the glacier. As I had ascended in the early morning light, an avalanche had swept the face and now a clean slope led down a relatively safe shaded area. With a little help from the occasional high-speed glissade through the snow, I whooshed down the slope and out into Camp II two hours after leaving the top.

Darkness settled in and the oval shimmering world of head-light reality led me down the homeward trail to Camp I. A few more tents had sprouted at Camp II, climbers having spent the day making the move up from Camp I en route to the top. Crampons crunched quietly through camp and the route dropped off into the gorge. Stars popped out and with no danger of falling in a crevasse or off a cliff, or having to spend the night out, I collapsed into the snow for a rest, my legs shaking with fatigue. With water and food finished at the top, camp soon drew me on. At a final rest above Camp I, the voices filtered up of campers snug in their sleeping bags. The Southern Cross appeared for the first time, set between two rock pillars on the ridge of the gorge. Like a good luck omen it guided my footsteps back to the tent. Twenty hours after leaving the tent I crawled back through the door and collapsed into the sleep of the dead.

CHAPTER 8

BUENOS AIRES ALPINISM

I woke after a deep, dreamless sleep. Clouds streaked the horizon, heralding the return of the bad weather. I said a quick silent prayer of thanks for sneaking through the weather window, the one day in two weeks blessed with a perfectly clear 24 hours. Over breakfast, thoughts turned to the creature comforts of Mendoza and Buenos Aires. Visions of life below had been avoided on the climb, acclimatising to the mountain environment being as important as acclimatising to the altitude. But now the bistros of Mendoza beckoned, with espresso coffees and small toasted cheese sandwiches served in the sunny sidewalk cafés.

We packed up and headed down that afternoon, passing a North American RMI guided group toiling up the glacier, packs heavy with two weeks of provisions for the higher camps. In the end they'd be working far harder than me to reach the summit and I was happy to be on my own, cut free from any group and its plodding requirements of tasteless freeze-dried food and endless load carries from camp to camp broken only by group politics and group decision sessions.

At Base Camp, Guillermo was on the radio for mules. They were on their way as per schedule, with arrival in two days' time. Guillermo invited himself and his sausages to dinner, requisitioning our frying pan to cook up his family's special spaghetti, a heady combination of the last of our fresh foods: garlic shaved thin, olives pitted and sliced, tomatoes stewed, bay leaves waved over the top. The combination simmered and popped, wafting the smells of a fine Italian restaurant about the tepee. To make it complete we cracked the bottle of red wine supplied by Raoul's *bodega* and finished the evening on coffee and a small cup of Glenfiddich. It was good to be back, especially with memories of sunset from the top of South America.

Morning dawned late. Base Camp was growing, first a group led by the Everest summiter and guide Phil Erschler, then guide Jim Williams and friend Sandy Pittman, all intent on Aconcagua as one of the Seven Summits. The concept of the Seven Summits had grown in popularity at an astounding rate, supporting international guides trailing well-heeled clients around the globe. Many of these were ridiculed by climbers who felt successful business people were simply buying into a well-controlled adventure and an easy route to the top. Having found a number of new friends amongst the clients and shared camps and meals with them around the world, I found most had been very successful at making money, often by novel entrepreneurial means, and then getting bored, had moved onto the physical and spiritual adventures found in the mountains. The Seven Summits gave them a recognisable goal, something both they and their peers could relate to, while still being a difficult and rarely achieved international adventure.

The well-known British mountaineer Doug Scott also wandered into camp, pitching a tiny tent for himself and his partner. Snowed out of Patagonia, he'd moved north to climb Aconcagua. He moved with a quiet efficiency that set him apart from the guided parties moving willy-nilly about camp. We shared a cup of tea, trading stories from Everest and about mutual friends, before Joe and I headed down the trail and back to civilisation. The three-day walk in would be reduced to a two-day walk out, a bone-numbing, river-hopping marathon weaving down the rocky river valley. It was the kind of distance that from the head of the valley looked more like a long drive, let alone a walk. But with the summit completed, spirits were high and guided the steps in a quick trot down the trail; I was already looking forward to Kilimanjaro.

Ricardo was at the trail head, his big creaking American car roaring off down the road at a frightening speed after days spent at mule pace. He ushered us to his home in an expansive out-of-season ski lodge, tossed us towels and a beer. The next hour was spent draining the hot water tanks dry, enjoying the first hot shower in two weeks. The sensation of water coursing over the skin and being clean was like uncovering a new body under the old, washing away the mountaineer for the return to civilisation.

The Claridge Hotel in Buenos Aires had been recommended by Norbu Tenzing, son of Tenzing Norgay who'd made the first ascent of Everest with Ed Hillary. Working for the travel company Mountain Travel-Sobek, he had been helping us with contacts on the Seven Summits. We had no desire to search out pensions in Buenos Aires after our time in the hills, so the five-star Argentinian opulence of a classic central city hotel complete with an oak bar and room service was soon home. Joe rushed off to organise a new passport and I faxed Norbu: 'Stuck here with hotel bill already grander than Aconcagua, can you help?' Norbu contacted the management and we became VIP guests at packaged tour rates.

Buenos Aires' bright lights and shops were like walking into a circus after the quiet of the mountain. But the mountain was as hard to shake off as the city had been; we were walking every-where at breakneck pace and waking every morning to look out the window at the weather. European designer shops sprouted from arcades and suited businessmen strolled the avenues, mobile phones and leather briefcases in hand. Restaurants were small and con-vivial; dark wooden panels, antique bars and locals curious about our travels abounded. Despite our mountain food, I'd lost a stone and was happy to eat my way through four meals and never less than one steak a day, although the city sophistication now allowed South Atlantic fish to surface, if only on the bottom corner of most menus. New jeans and T-shirts set us up for nights out and the migration to Africa. Four days after we arrived, Joe finally extracted a new passport from the American Embassy and we rode down the tree-lined avenues for the last time and out to the airport.

'No *señor*, no pass,' said the crisply uniformed customs agent, taking Joe's passport. 'Buenos Aires,' and he pointed back to the city. Did he want a bribe, I wondered? We waited. Flight time approached. A manager for the airline approached as we began to panic.

'You need a stamp in your passport,' he told Joe. 'With a new passport, you haven't officially entered Argentina and you can't leave until you've entered.'

'Great,' said Joe, 'where do I get that?'

'It's okay,' he said, 'we have an arrangement with customs here. Come with me and we'll get it stamped and you'll be on the plane.'

We'd been rescued just in time, last call echoing through the sound system. I took the cameras and got on the plane. Joe returned as the doors shut, just squeezing through them as the gangway pulled back.

We were off to Miami, London, Nairobi and Kilimanjaro. I settled back with a celebratory glass of champagne to look out the window towards the Andes. Where were those guanacos?

III
AFRICA

CHAPTER 9

LONDON, NAIROBI, MOSHI

CONTINENT HOPPING. THE winged aluminium tubes whisked out of South America, through North America, dropped into London, skimmed over Europe, and made a final stop in Africa. Joe and I had traversed four of the world's seven continents in as many days. If only the climbs were as easy.

The taxi-driver from central London to Heathrow Airport was good-humoured about the seven bags stacked in his cab. 'This must be an adventure,' he commented, 'do you carry *all* this to the top?' as he stacked the duffle bags and camera cases into the front, back and boot of his cab. The odour of mule still pervaded the duffles. I wondered what they would smell like at the end of the year.

London faded in the fog below. The 747 was full, Joe relegated to the main deck while upstairs I had a TV producer and an aid worker for company. It was soon dark outside. The close and comfortable atmosphere of the small room divorced us from the cabin below and an efficient bar service trundling the short reaches of the aisle soon made us close friends. Dawn broke as we hit the tarmac in Nairobi. The hotel didn't quite match service in the air. 'Your room will be ready at noon, that is check-in time, that is when your room will be ready.' The bags were stacked in the corner and we went for a five-hour breakfast. This was Africa but it hadn't registered yet. At noon we retreated to the airy room with starched white sheets and soft mattresses, the first real bed in five days of travel since leaving Buenos Aires.

The fog of a London winter still clouded the lungs, the duffle bags smelled like South America and the breezes were out of Africa, while London taxi receipts littered the bedside table. It was Friday. I should be heading off full of enthusiasm to the tallest mountain on the continent, but my body and mind said differently — we shall sleep. A London flu took hold of us and a feverish rush of insecurity set in, huddled in a hotel room somewhere in the middle of Africa, the snows of Kilimanjaro forgotten.

By Sunday, life had returned. A local climbing guide stopped by for coffee and went over the map with us. With nothing arranged in advance, the basics — getting across Kenya, shopping for food, where to hire porters — all had to be planned. The guide quickly put us on the right track: 'Take the bus from here. Talk to several companies when you get to Tanzania. I wouldn't recommend going anywhere near the glaciers on Kili, most have receded to the extent they are a 1,000-metre rubble heap at their base, 500 metres of black ice and then a maze of crevasses. The climbing isn't even hard, just very dangerous with lots of loose rock.' So we made our plans: get on the bus and get out of Nairobi, then take the next step.

As we walked around Nairobi, the city felt like it had no heart. High-rises with shacks next door were interspersed with colonial British office buildings. Nairobi's history, rising as it did from the plain in a no-man's-land between the Masai and Kikuyu tribes, had long made it a city of migrants, even after the British took over following World War I. Gaining its independence in 1963, it remains a collection of tribal, European and Asian cultures awash in a city which people seem to treat more as a way station than a home. Nearly everything seemed transient, quickly built and quickly dispensed with. At night the metal shutters came down on the shop doors and the people huddled inside or scuttled from place to place with hunched shoulders and a hurried gait.

The bus left at 7 a.m., on time, which I mention because it is an oddity in such places. The bus was full of a mix of white and black, a European and African hodge-podge of cultures and languages in a sleepy early morning banter, searching for common ground on the three-hour ride to Tanzania. Once the edge of town was reached fifteen minutes later, Nairobi rapidly disappeared from view and mind, replaced by rolling plains and solitary trees sprouting from the horizon. The hot dry air from the world's hottest continent washed in the windows as the bus rolled along the black strip of asphalt, heat waves rising like airborne hills in the road ahead. A single faded white stripe marked the centre, the road edge fading off into reddish dirt with the plains appearing as a wave of colour. The trees grew in size and spread like green leafy mushrooms ten metres above their roots.

A tree alongside the road moved and a giraffe walked out from beneath it, exposing its gangly legs and neck arcing skyward like an oversized tree branch. Life outside a zoo made them real, a part of the earth, their immense height placing them at home in the tall trees, their legs effortlessly carrying them over the brush and rocks below. Their colours in a zoo make them stand out like punk rockers. But in the wild, amongst the mottled shade of the trees against the backdrop of orange earth and plain, they simply blended in, a natural part of the environment.

The next patch of low bush yielded a flock of ostriches, pecking sporadically at the ground and looking over their shoulders suspiciously. As the bus drew close they kicked into a run, their legs carrying them up and over the brush in long bounds. Africa, the dark continent, appeared anything but dark. Creatures that boggled the imagination strolled along the roadside, making humanity a sideshow. The animals had suddenly switched roles, looking at us behind the glass windows on the bus as we passed through their homeland, just as we peered at them in zoos.

Low rolling hills covered with dark scrubby trees loomed out of the plains ahead as the bus rolled up to the Kenya-Tanzania border. A collection of low tin huts selling bright beads and baskets lined the road leading up to a squat grey guardhouse. We filed out of the bus and in one door, were scrutinised by a swarthy black man, passed onto another, forms were filled out, stamps pounded with authority into our passports, and out we went the other door — and out of Kenya. The bus drove 100 metres and the show was repeated — welcome to Tanzania. Despite inefficiency and the obvious effects of a burdensome and boring job on the officials, there was still that tension endemic in border crossings, knowing that if something goes wrong, it will go badly wrong. Back on the bus, safe from the scowling officials, we pulled away in a roar, leaving the hawkers of coloured beads and necklaces with their hands half in and half out of the windows in a last desperate sale. The beggars of Nairobi had been dirty and depressing, the city eating away their humanity. The country was obviously poor, but released from the city, people were much more enthusiastic, joking and pointing at my ears and their ears, indicating I needed at least one set of earrings, if not the ten they all wore at once, to make a fashion statement in Tanzania. My complete lack of jewellery, since I only ever wore a watch, was a challenge to them. I could have traded the watch for a set of necklaces that would have stacked up to the bottom of my chin, but with the beads having a distinct resemblance to local rocks with a bit of Coke bottle thrown in, it may not have been particularly wise.

During the day, clouds had built up in the east, high in the sky, bulking up against the height of Kilimanjaro, obscuring it from view when the bus finally passed close below it on the journey south. The plains had changed to dark, brush-covered hills, the breezes cooled from the dry, sweat-producing heat of the prairie. The bus pulled to a halt in a ramshackle village of rotting concrete buildings and wooden shacks. Everybody got off except Joe and me, the only passengers going to Moshi at the base of Kilimanjaro. We were heading for Africa's last outpost as we curved around the base of the mountain, for the final hour. Kilimanjaro dominated the land, sweeping north in a barely distinguishable curve, disappearing into the dark green, almost black forest lining the road, before fading completely in the mist above.

Below the highway, dusty lanes stretched off along shallow gullies, lined with lazy fences meandering down into the scrubby forest. Goats wandered over the hillocks and skinny cows stood flicking their tails in the heat. Everywhere people lolled in the doors of huts or clustered together in the shade on the porches of rambling houses. A sure sign of wealth was a broken-down car close by, from an era of bygone extravagance. The land exuded the aura of overworked and underproducing earth, then a coffee farm would sprout up, the bushes growing strong and green in the heat. Obviously the money was in the coffee beans. The farms grew closer together and the bus swung into Moshi, which could only be described as a two-horse town. We found the best hotel, took the only room with a shower, made ample use of the cold water and collapsed into an early bed. White sheets with no blankets provided a more than adequate covering. Kilimanjaro rested above, wreathed in clouds, the occasional breath of mountain air playing through the window as darkness settled.

CHAPTER 10

LAND ROVERS AND LEOPARDS

AT DAWN, THE SUN came across the land and into the window, slanting across the room with equatorial brightness, as close to the land as the earth would allow it. A rooster crowed loudly outside the window, having been warming up since 4 a.m. The voices of people getting up in the farms echoed over the fields, the clang of pots and calls from room to room, no doubt 'Have you seen my shoes?' in Swahili.

Out the window was a clear and cloudless day. Through the dark tree branches was the immense bulk of Kilimanjaro. It rose and rose, squares of green and brown field leading to dark forest, rock just coming awake in the sun, then the icefields, shining like mirrors against the blue of the sky. It was too big, too immense to feel like a normal mountain. Most mountains are part of a range, with foothills and ridges leading the eye upwards. Kilimanjaro rose out of an immense plain extending on all sides and went up and up, with no break or change. Three degrees south of the equator, 30 kilometres separated hot brown plains from icefields hanging off the summit plateau. Kilimanjaro wasn't supported by lesser peaks or built slowly. It challenged the eye to take it all in at once.

Step one, get to Moshi, was accomplished. Step two, find some porters and transport to the peak. The company recommended to us had an office in a hotel in Moshi, located in little more than a wide hallway, a single piece of wood panelling separating reception from the main room. A short man with a large stomach sat back in a rickety wooden chair, the springs squeaking with annoyance. 'Yes, I can get you to Kilimanjaro, with a Land Rover and four porters and a head porter. I can get you to any side. I can arrange your food. I can pick you up. I can arrange hotel, where are you staying?'

It was obvious this man could arrange anything; it was only a matter of price. We wanted to go to the far side of the mountain, the Western Breach, which few people visited and was as far away as possible from the normal route. Finding a difficult climbing route to ascend on Kilimanjaro sounded more trouble than it was worth. A morning spent eyeing the peak through binoculars had verified what the Nairobi mountain guide had described — a mountain experiencing serious glacial recession with acres of poor and rotting rock. The Western Breach at least allowed a less-travelled route, weaving its way through a series of rocky cliffs to the summit, away from the hordes that frequented the normal trail.

The fat man was sweating and wiping his forehead on the long tail of his shirt. He scribbled notes on random pieces of paper and punched the keys of a digital calculator occupying pride of place in the centre of his ramshackle desk. 'Two thousand two hundred dollars,' he said with an expansive smile and a wave of his hands, as if blessing us with the deal of the century. We argued him down to $1,800 with an agreement to change another US$1,000 with him.

The black market thrives in Tanzania; highly illegal, but with a premium of over 100 percent on the bank rates, experienced travellers are rarely seen in a bank. The requirement for receipts is normally forgotten at the border and even these can be purchased, with black market cash, for the worried traveller concerned about the border bandits dressed as custom officials. The black market kept all local costs at less than half an already cheap price, making day-to-day living practically free. Like any country that tries to control its currency, Tanzania had failed miserably, creating a second economy further distancing the haves from the have nots. In an attempt to create greater social equality, the government succeeded only in keeping one of the world's poorest countries at the bottom of the heap.

Moshi yielded up four food shops with enthusiastic displays of the latest in canned goods in their dirty windows. Inside, shelves were stacked sparsely with the latest shipment, rarely selling anything from the window. Most of the display cans were empty, a historical journey through the best the store had to offer since time eternal with no basis in reality. It was as if a year's supply of one thing came in every two years, leaving a store stocked with ten times as many cans of diced carrots as they would ever sell, while a broad supply of the basics was impossible to find. A visit to all four stores finally yielded a small tin of jam, as fresh bread seemed to be freely available and our UK-purchased peanut butter needed something to keep it off the roofs of our mouths.

Food seemed to be abundant but nothing went together. Bread rolls were everywhere, butter, honey or meat was non-existent. Chunky sugar came in dirty brown bags. Instant coffee didn't exist in a country famous for its coffee. Fresh fruit in the stores looked tired and often the victim of having travelled long distances, but stallholders out on the road picked it from the fields behind them and sold it for next to nothing. Everything seemed to be packed in aid boxes with 'For local distribution only, not for sale' printed in red letters next to the initials and symbol of the International Red Cross and the United Nations logo.

We'd have the benefit of four porters to carry food, so weight wasn't a problem. Our head porter, Peter, arrived in the afternoon. His calf muscles bulged out of his traditional, just-below-the-knee climbing breeches and biceps filled the arms of his white T-shirt, red 'Le Sportif' logo gracing the front. His quiet confident manner and quick wit suited our mini-expedition perfectly.

'Tomorrow we'll travel by Land Rover to the end of the road, then walk a few miles to the camp. The next day we walk up to High Camp at 4,800 metres. You'll need to get up very early to reach the summit before it clouds over.' I was becoming used to the African way of talking, of smiling sadly when it looked like something wouldn't work out, as if fate had taken control but it should be accepted. Peter had worked on Kilimanjaro since his youth, with ascents of the peak 'somewhere around 80'. Having a good head porter could make the difference between a successful and a potentially disastrous climb. Overseeing four other porters, he'd be in charge of decisions if the weather got bad or anything out of the ordinary happened on our trek in. Kilimanjaro wouldn't provide a climbing challenge, but mountains always throw up something interesting when least expected and this was exactly what would happen on Kilimanjaro.

By evening, plans in place, we found Africa comfortable for the first time since arrival. The jump from South America had looked good on paper, but the hop from one culture to another, with a few nights in London in between, had caused a serious dose of culture shock. With the familiarity of the mountain ahead, it was the first time since descending from Aconcagua that life felt normal.

The rooster was back on duty the next morning, pre-empting any need for an alarm clock. We dragged the duffle down the stairs and sat staring at our greasy eggs and lukewarm coffees as the sun came up. A cool breeze blew off the mountain, hovering outside in another clear day. The Land Rover bounced up, of indescribable vintage, looking worn but hopefully not worn out. The porters greeted us with enthusiasm, their smattering of English laced with Swahili a reminder how far we were from home. With duffles strapped on the roof, the Land Rover clanked to life and set off, gears grinding and engine popping, circling the town square and speeding off down the highway back the way we had come into town two days previously.

'This man is my brother,' said Peter, 'and this man, my cousin, and this man my cousin's wife's father, uncle I think? This man, well, this man is almost like brother, but friend, only married to my sister.' We were obviously on a family outing. It wouldn't be the ideal situation if nepotism was a concern, but each of the men, ranging in age from 19 to 63, was quick to follow Peter's orders and enthusiastic about the journey, smiling broadly and chattering amongst themselves, obviously happy for the work. The porters would get $7 a day and Peter would get twice that.

An hour later the Land Rover turned off the main highway and headed north on a single lane of asphalt, traversing square blocks of farmland. Kilimanjaro rose up like a friendly behemoth above the road, a clean sweep of land rising to the summit. Drawing closer it gained shape, perfect concentric circles formed into valleys and ridges; cliffs stood out in relief and individual glaciers rose out of the mass of glistening white ice. The mountain's personality was surfacing at last. The asphalt soon faded, the driver slowing and finally stopping to pop the hubs into four-wheel drive. If Moshi was a two-horse town, we now entered a half-a-horse town. Peter cautioned us to not wander off. 'It is not really dangerous, but you have many things, these people have few things, some of them do not think it is fair.' Keeping close to Peter we headed off to buy a huge bunch of green bananas. 'Dinner,' said Peter. 'You like bananas?' I did, but was not sure I wanted to eat a bunch of green ones. 'Oh, we cook them,' added Peter, sensing my distaste.

The town had one street, warped wooden boardwalks, the ubiquitous Coke sign, but no Cokes. Behind windows, woman and children peered from the shadows at us. The men lounged on the steps, eyeing us suspiciously. It was obvious the route was little travelled by Europeans — or any whites for that matter, our colour standing out like white dots in a sea of black ink. I felt how minorities must feel everywhere, alone and isolated. I tried to tell myself, 'I'm just another colour, it makes no difference,' but still felt completely alien.

I wasn't the only one feeling out of place. Back in the Land Rover and headed up the hill, Peter said, 'This side of Kilimanjaro is very different, the people are hard, they don't like foreigners, even I am a foreigner here. None of them can read, they see no television, the outside world is a bad place and anything from that place is bad. But don't worry, the mountain is beautiful this side, very rare, no one comes here. We leave the bad people behind.' The distrust amongst the different tribes obviously still ran strong, no matter where the colonists had drawn their boundaries.

The road soon turned to rough gravel, the fields grew sparse and the Land Rover finally pulled up at a stick across the road held up by a fence going nowhere. A village of small wooden shacks, like something out of a Western movie, dotted the hillside. Fields of grass and small paddocks with pigs and chickens were set behind the shacks, the chickens scratching sporadically in the dust. Peter went inside one hut, papers were stamped, hands were shaken, the ranger came out and peered at Joe and me and nodded. The gate was ceremoniously raised and we passed into the park.

'We must watch out for leopards,' said Peter. 'The Chief Ranger says a leopard wandered through the village recently. They may be at our camp.' The surrounding forest grew thick and impenetrable as we gained altitude, leopards undoubtedly hiding in the shadows. 'And lions too,' said Peter. 'The ladies, you know, the lioness, she is not the woman you would want to meet on your own,' he laughed and made an outlandish high-pitched scream. 'You hear that, you are dead,' he said and grabbed my arm. The other porters were laughing loudly. I never was sure whether there were leopards, lions, or neither of the above. Just what I needed, to be attacked by a leopard while climbing Kilimanjaro. It sounded very brave and romantic, but looking into the deep forest and dark brush, I had no desire to leave the Land Rover or the phalanx of porters.

Characteristically, the engine conked out on the biggest hill, the Land Rover coming to a coughing halt. The driver disappeared under the bonnet, wrench in hand, muttering and cursing. 'It is late, the Land Rover will not go up any more hills, he says,' said Peter, motioning to the driver. I could see the driver working up to a point where he could dump us alongside the road, adding an extra day or two to the climb, just so he could get home early. Having paid a premium of $800 to visit this side of the mountain, I wasn't about to be left to hike up the road. It was difficult to know whether the softly, softly approach or the ultimatum was best. I remembered the blunt and overriding manner of the short, fat man in Moshi who had organised our transport and decided anybody he hired probably wouldn't want to deal with him if they didn't do what he said. 'Tell the driver,' I said to Peter, 'that if the

Land Rover won't go any further, we will ride back down to Moshi with him, straight to the office and then get a new Land Rover and driver to bring us back up here tomorrow.' The driver's head came out from under the bonnet. He glared at Peter. Then he glared at me. For good measure he retreated back under the bonnet waving the wrench for another minute. Then he emerged, pronounced the engine fixed and we loaded up again and set out up the hill. I saw him start the engine, it sputtered and he slid the choke in, obviously the cause of the problem in the first place. It was an old trick that seemed to identify third world countries where drivers tired long before their vehicles did.

The forest turned to brush and then low scrub as the track wound in endless S-turns up the plateau. The engine ground on as we climbed into the red and orange volcanic earth of Kilimanjaro's slopes. The road ended abruptly in a sandy circular patch of orange. The driver unceremoniously dumped our bags off the roof and turned and headed down the hill in a cloud of dust without even a wave goodbye.

We were cast adrift on the side of Kilimanjaro, the long ride and sudden departure leaving us feeling stranded. As if sensing how I felt, Peter patted me on the back and said, 'Don't forget, here there be leopards,' and grinned widely. It looked like there could be. 'Come, the hut is just over the hill, we have an easy day and a big dinner,' said Peter. The porters lifted the duffles effortlessly and with them balanced lightly on the crowns of their heads, set off up an indistinct trail heading across the plateau. With leopards leaping from the shadows, I quickly threw on my pack and followed them. The sides of Kilimanjaro rolled over hummocks and into miniature valleys, skirted small cliffs and led to a hillock set close against the rising slope. The slopes were cut by age-old volcanic rivers streaming down the sides of the peak, leaving a rippled and rolled surface; it was like ascending a steep river of brightly covered rock rolling down from the heights.

Perched above the cliffs was a steel hut, the roof a set of metal panels cut into thin triangles that extended out to form a circular structure, 10 metres round. A quick glance verified a fire-blackened interior, trash stacked and fuming in one corner. We retreated to a nearby sandy patch to pitch the tent. Camp was at 3,600 metres and the summit still over 2,200 vertical metres higher. With the sun shining straight into the face, the crags stood out, towering orange and red cliffs cut by icy white glaciers. The face looked bigger and steeper than the photographs, framed by the glaciers, the towering icicles of the Breach Icefall streaming like tears from the summit icefield onto the Heim Glacier. The upper reaches of the peak looked immense and the view through the binoculars only heightening the terrain. The sun burned off into the horizon directly in front of the tent, fading below the bulk of Mt Meru, a 4,500-metre volcanic cone that rose as a shadowed monolith from the plains, like a small mirror image of Kilimanjaro in the distance.

'Bananas,' shouted Peter from the hut, 'hot bananas.' A huge bunch of small green bananas had been boiling away in a large kettle ever since we'd arrived. I peeled back the dark and shrunken skin, revealing the pulp. It was sweet and cloying, but tasted like it must be healthy. The porters were eating them by the dozens; I settled for three bananas and Joe, wisely, opted not to try them. We retreated to our own tent for spaghetti while the bananas rumbled in my stomach. The sun set in a red ball, sliding down between the clouds, streaks of late afternoon sun sliding through in rays to spotlight patches of Kilimanjaro.

There was a scuffle outside the tent just as I settled into my sleeping bag and Peter's face appeared around the edge of the flap. 'Don't worry, I keep first watch, leopards hunt at night,' he said, grinning broadly. 'Sleep well.' I still couldn't decide if he was kidding.

CHAPTER 11

SANDS OF KILIMANJARO

THE FREEZING WIND at dawn on Aconcagua, the heat of the South American plains, the chill of a London fog, the blast of an African savannah and now the frost on the tent at dawn on Kilimanjaro. I rolled over and fired the stove for coffee before losing momentum. The air was crystal clear, the plains set in the morning light outside the tent door. Around the corner of the icy nylon Kilimanjaro loomed. The sun behind it set us deep in the morning shade. A light breeze swirled through the low brush and along the rolls of the volcanic streams, washing up and over the tent.

'Coffee?' I passed Joe's cup across. We'd both been getting used to Africa in slow stages and hadn't said much in days, travelling quietly in our own worlds, the details of travel filling our minds. Despite the closeness enforced by our day-to-day living, we got on very well together, Joe busy filming and photographing while I looked after travel details, food and the ascent of the mountain. The outside world was so consuming it left little time to think or worry about anything else. With common goals getting to, up and down the peaks and onto the next one, there was little time left for anything else.

The sun sloped up over the top of the peak and touched camp by 8 a.m., the porters wandering out of the hut 30 metres behind us. They seemed in no hurry to get going, the day's walk being a gentle trail from 3,600 to 4,800 metres with 15 kilometres to cover. The porridge bubbled away, followed by another coffee, by which time the porters had assembled outside the hut and Joe had set up the view camera to take a photograph. The view camera took a five by seven inch negative, resulting in prints of incredible clarity. The disadvantage was the camera, photo holders, tripod and cases weighed an extra 25 kilograms, an ungainly weight at the best of times. What with two video cameras, 35 mm cameras and a couple of small cameras for quick shots, I occasionally felt as if we could open a camera store at any of our stops if the budget ran low. This amount of equipment also required film, batteries and Hi-8 video-tapes, another suitcase in itself. Being an enthusiast of the travel-ling light and fast school, the gear would occasionally rise up and overwhelm my thoughts, but the bulk of it, for my sanity, was luckily Joe's responsibility. Setting up the view camera always created a theatrical atmosphere, the tripod, box and black sheet over Joe's head a return to the age when every photo was art. The porters assumed relaxed positions about the hut, their high-top sandshoes with toes sticking out the top and floppy pants setting them mid-way between a century past and a century that hadn't quite yet arrived.

By 10 a.m. we were on the trail, wandering across the plateau and up long sloping hills. Slowly the brush faded, to be replaced by orange rocks and moss-covered volcanic boulders. Lunch was underneath a towering outcrop several hundred metres high, in the shelter of a boulder forming an overhanging cave. Above, the mountain now rose in clean craggy lines, the terraces leading be-tween the cliffs evident as the route led to the summit plateau. To the right, the Breach icicles hung shining in the afternoon sun, tremendous falls of vertical ice cascading off the summit ice-fields. Bordered by towering black cliffs, they made a frightening sight, scene of many climbing stories. The guide in Nairobi thought they had been ascended only twice to date, and not for many years, the ice rotting and cracking with each progressive year, leaving little to climb and what was there no longer worth trying to hang onto. But the cascading sheets of ice didn't stop me dreaming about one day returning to discover a hidden route linking the ice and the rock to create a new path to Kilimanjaro's summit.

We climbed through 4,500 metres, the afternoon mists creeping down from the summit, sliding down the mountain like the grey plague. When the mist reached the porters in their dark clothing, they disappeared completely; only the red duffles showed faintly, floating along above the ground as if suspended. The day turned chill and frosty, small ice crystals floating in the air. The mist blocked the sun, dark and forbidding, and the trail disappeared just a few metres in front of my eyes. Rocks sprouted like monsters, dark and shadowy, then disappeared altogether. The mist moved in waves, then blew out as fast as it blew in on the last long hill into the high and final camp. The ground was rough and rocky, set in a small valley with cliffs rising above and falling away steeply below. A sign lay on the ground pointing over the hill to 'Arrow Hut, 16,300 feet, $1/2$ mile', but there was no reason to go there, the route leading straight up through the cliffs above. There was no one in sight and it was a desolate and windy place. The sun dropped into the plains and dinner was in the dark, as we threw a few snacks and a litre of water in the pack for the early morning departure. Kilimanjaro wasn't giving us any time off.

Three a.m. I rose to waves of nausea and green banana bile rising up in my throat. I felt very ill and nauseous and crawled outside the tent. A freezing wind swirled among the rocks. I stood in my socks, the sky black with stars as bright as the moon. The mountain rose as a dark heap behind the tent, ice-white glaciers running like fingers through the black rock. The air whispered thinly in and out of my lungs, feeling insufficient. A cold sweat rose and froze on my forehead. I wasn't well, the summit loomed, the dark menaced me with a chill air. My head reeled as I crawled back into the tent. I couldn't sleep. I knew I couldn't climb, but maybe a drink would help. The stove was a reassuring roar, a homely sound in a land far removed from anything I knew.

Herbal tea, a cup of porridge cooked and thrown out. The night grew colder. I lay back, still feeling nauseous. Joe stirred and I went to check on Peter, who'd be carrying Joe's cameras while he filmed. I set off in a daze, Joe and Peter illuminated with the video

light below. A few steps, a rest, then the nausea cleared to be replaced by a pounding headache. A ridge led upwards, the volcanic
rock sharp and solid but covered with light gravel sliding back
down the hill underfoot. It wasn't particularly steep, but looking
down, neither was it a place to slip off. Kilimanjaro now spread
out in all directions, the sheer cliffs of the Western Breach to the
right and a glacier-clad ridge sweeping out to the left. Dawn was a
strip of colour sneaking around the side of the mountain to light
up the plains of Africa. The air was cold and crisp, breezes wafting
off the glaciers. The sun hit the volcanic cone of Mt Meru and
swept down it, bathing it in a hot white light, while the shadow of
Kilimanjaro shrunk on the plains. At 5.30 a.m. it was pitch black
and at 6 a.m. the bright light of morning covered the continent.
On the Western Breach it would be hours before the sun hit directly, sheltered as it was amongst the towering cliffs. The cliff grew
steeper but the route wound through gentle terraces, a maze of
sharply etched boulders in huge stacks, like square pasta cut from
a mould and dumped from the top of Africa down Kilimanjaro's
sides.

Slowly the headache faded, the lungs cleared, the stomach settled. More water and no food created a delicate equilibrium that
seemed to be winning the green banana and altitude war. The day
was moving quickly and the mountain growing, one terrace leading to the next, rock piled on top of rock, the rim of the volcano
hovering above, closer around one corner and then fading back
behind another. The cliffs towered like mammoth vertical orange
and yellow dominoes, one stacked atop another. The blocks were
clean-cut and angular, a fairytale of gigantic shapes cleaved from
the rock. The rock ended abruptly, a final cliff towered, the route
snuck between yellow and orange and red towers and popped suddenly out on the rim.

The ground changed immediately: rocky cliff below, fine gravel
and sand on the summit plateau, feet sinking into powdery puffs
of fine volcanic dust. The rim rolled away, dipping to the left, before rising in a long slow circle several kilometres away then disap-

pearing from sight on the opposite side behind a snowfield. To the right, the rim loomed up steeply over a rounded hill, then dropped and rose again to the summit, a bump on the far right horizon. But most amazing was the dry summit plateau with ice-fields rising vertically 30 metres straight up out of the sand. It was half Sahara desert and half Antarctic ice-field, perched on the edge of the African plains. A trace of mist rose up the cliff, heralding the afternoon clouds that would soon follow.

The route cut across the bottom of the ice-field, the only trace of snow we touched on Kilimanjaro, and set off up the final rise to the summit. The gravel crunched underfoot and the sun shone down warmly. Every step opened up a new vista. The ice-fields laced the inside of the crater like monster cobwebs, creeping and crawling in long spirals across the huge plateau before sneaking off the summit in long tendrils dripping out of sight into the cliffs below. The mists grew rapidly, building off the sides of Kilimanjaro and rising up towards the summit, like they were trying to sweep the glaciers back up into the sky. The wind blew puffs of air, rising on all sides of the crater and spilling over into its depths. Then the mist would clear, disappearing as fast as it had arrived.

I crested the final hummock on the rim and saw a pile of rocks and flags marking the summit. It was an easy stroll along the gravel-strewn rim to the top, the crater falling away steeply to the left and the ice-field on the right framing the drop back into Tanzania. A metre-high rock marked the top of Africa. After the morning's struggle, the climb had become very pleasant, the sun warm and welcoming, the summit breeze fresh but not strong. The mists had held off long enough to give a clear 360-degree view. The blue directly above faded to the white of the horizon, then to the brown of the plains. Closer, the brown of the plains deepened, heat haze rose and the tilled fields in Kilimanjaro's rich soil formed patchwork quilts of dark greens and browns, finally fading into the near-black of the mountain forests, the red rock of the ridges rising out of them and cleaving the glaciers. It was a microcosm of world geography on a massive scale.

The mists rose up in another wave, enveloping me, then faded away to reveal Joe and Peter cresting the rim below, the only other people in sight. Even the hordes that ascend the opposite side were nowhere to be seen. I had a last spin around, Africa circling my feet, and set off back down the mountain. I was more relieved than excited at reaching the top after starting the day feeling like I couldn't move, let alone climb Kilimanjaro. After any summit, though, there was the clear-cut feeling of accomplishment, of having set out to do something and completing it.

Kilimanjaro had been more exciting than difficult, the summit climb taking only five hours, with two hours on top and several hours to wander back down the hill. The mists rose as if on cue as I reached the cliff and started down, swirling about like a thick fog, blocking out the sun. The wind grew cold. The mountain seemed more like a mountain now, less a morning stroll, the day's rapid ascent of 1,200 metres, followed by a drop back to the high camp and a further descent, beginning to look like a long climb. The route wove down through the cliffs and slid down the final slope into camp.

The porters, disliking the high altitude and spartan conditions at the high camp, had moved camp down into the forest below, a descent of three more hours. Joe and I hadn't liked the idea of a long descent at the end of a summit climb, and this also meant the porters had carried everything we normally carried, plus Peter's load. They were obviously very strong. But carrying 40-kilogram duffles around on their heads down rocky, root-strewn and muddy tracks didn't seem much fun, no matter how confident they were. With only a threadbare goat-hair blanket for the three of them to curl up under at night, they couldn't have been very warm. It was easy to see why a camping holiday next to a glacier at 4,800 metres wasn't terribly pleasant and why they'd want to get to lower altitudes with firewood and warmer temperatures.

We'd chosen to ascend the west side of Kilimanjaro, follow the same route up and down from the high camp to the summit and then to cut around and descend the Umbwe trail, the steepest route on the south side of Kilimanjaro. This would allow us to experience as much of the mountain as possible and avoid the most used trails.

It was 3 p.m. when we set out down from the high camp, rolling through rock troughs and over the glacial terminus stacked with loose boulders. The mist melted in the late afternoon sun and the trail led steeply around the towering Southwest Face of Kilimanjaro, the day turning warm and wonderful. The landscape changed dramatically as the trail descended, dropping into the upper reaches of the forest. There was low scraggy brush and what looked like miniature palm trees, spiked trunks and tight balls of leaves spiralling in all directions from the top, sprouted from the ridge tops and clustered in the valleys. The mountain returned to the terrain we'd experienced on the way up; the distinctive volcanic ripples meant we were walking down the rapids and rolls of a river set in stone.

A final sweeping corner loomed and another distinctive round steel hut swept into view, sprouting from the forest, perched on the edge of a steep green gorge. We stood suspended in the light, the dark forests below. The sun tipped the tops of ridges as they descended in long lines from the top of Kilimanjaro. The ice-fields glowed dull orange in the final light. The top seemed years away, separated from the lower slopes by experiences that hovered outside a normal time-frame, the summit attached more to the heavens above than to the earth below.

I drifted into a nap, only to find Peter shaking me. 'Robert, Robert, I'm sorry, my uncle is hurt, it's his knee. Maybe you can look at it?' That was the end of a perfect climb.

CHAPTER 12

UNCLE PORTER

WITH DUSK DESCENDING, it was nearly dark inside the steel hut, only a flame of orange sunset leaking through the cracks in the wall. The air was heavy with stale smoke and the ground pounded hard underfoot from previous climbers. Three of the porters clustered around one corner, talking amongst themselves and casting glances over their shoulders. The uncle lay on a low bench, his leg extended in front of him, streaks of tears smudged through the dust on his face. I felt his leg and realised he had no kneecap. Around the knee was inflamed. I ran my hand over his leg and finally found the kneecap, about a third of the way up his thigh. His knee was so stiff and painful it must have been out of joint as well. The only good thing was everything seemed internal and, while he was in lots of pain, it looked as though it was isolated to the knee area and hopefully hadn't cut any major blood vessels inside. The best I could offer were plenty of my private supply of very strong pain pills. What he needed was a hospital.

Joe had pitched the tent when I returned and the stove was bubbling. I got out the map and we sat down with Peter. We'd planned on taking an additional two days to walk out down the long trail to the road. The route had sounded romantic in the guide: 'It is a serious route, unsuitable for the solitary or the inexperienced.' This now seemed like the worst possible place to be. I'd carried enough people off mountains in stretchers to know anything less than a road is a nightmare to move people down. It was a good 25 kilometres and 2,000 metres of vertical descent to the road. The trails had been good enough, but never more than a foot wide. Cliffs with steep drops on each side and heavy bush were evident just leaving camp.

'Let's sleep,' was all I could decide. 'Tomorrow we'll work this out. Don't worry, Peter, we'll work this out together.'

Joe and I had both grown to admire Peter's enthusiasm and sense of humour. He'd quickly gone from worrying about our every step and directing our steps as he often had to do with tourists on the regular route, to showing us the more difficult and spectacular shortcuts and racing us up and down the steep sandy slopes. Faced with an injured porter, I wanted to let him know we now wouldn't revert to a client/porter relationship, leaving him in the hills with his uncle. Any 63-year-old man who carried a 30-kilogram duffle on his head for $7 a day had our respect as a fellow climber. Peter thanked us profusely, but it probably didn't help his sleep. The world could have caved in on me that night, I slept like a baby.

Dawn, beautifully sculpted, erupted over the ridge with a suddenness only an equatorial existence allows. Perched next to the hut on the edge of the dark tropical gorge below, with Kilimanjaro rearing up from the back window, we were very close to heaven. The sun was already warm, the air crisp. Then I remembered Uncle Porter, as I'd come to call him, unable to pronounce his name properly. The only sign of civilisation was a thin wisp of smoke far below us floating up from the edge of the forest. It was going to be a very long day.

First, we had to decide what to do. In the end, it was really quite simple. Uncle Porter had to be carried out, on our backs. The trail was too narrow and steep to use a stretcher; helicopters didn't exist. The faster we got him out the better. One day if possible. I had an extra cup of coffee. Uncle Porter had looked fairly slight compared to the other porters, but having to suddenly put him on my back, he felt like a giant. With a body toughened by years of farming and carrying loads, his body was strong and wiry, a solid 12-stone load, 76 kilograms. A normal heavy load would be 40 kilos in the mountains. Would any of us even be able to walk with a load like that on our backs, not to mention down a very rough trail, around huge roots and through narrow passages barely a body width wide? I'd splinted his leg with a partially inflated Therma-rest pad, a compromise between completely isolating it with the maximum protection and still allowing some movement when it was inevitably bumped. Better for a minimal amount of twisting than to snap it in half altogether! Two more pain pills started his day, then I strapped him inside the pack. Lifted to my feet with a porter on each side, I took the first staggering step of the day. I could see the porters were sceptical, but felt if I could get us off to a good start with a half-hour carry, we could keep up the momentum. Hopefully, with their combination of pride in their own strength and respect for the uncle, we'd manage to get him down.

I tottered through the first steps, almost tripping. Carrying 12 stone on my back required an immediate adjustment in balance. Bend over too far and the load was liable to fly over my head. Back too far and we'd land in a heap on the ground. Bend a knee too far and I would collapse in an ungainly pile. All the while the shattered right leg hung under my right arm, dangling uselessly, yet catching on every branch and piece of brush alongside the trail. Five minutes later, I'd adopted a slow but steady pace. It had little to do with physical ability, the weight being absurd. After ten minutes I realised my call for 30-minute carries had been outrageously over-optimistic. I already felt like I'd climbed Kilimanjaro twice. Thighs burned, knees were ready to buckle and the weight was compressing my spine out the base of my back. Every minute crawled on my watch, sweat poured off my forehead. At 15 minutes I allowed myself a minute's rest, leaning sideways on a rock. Attempts to protect Uncle's leg from bumps were impossible, the sharp intake of breath between his teeth indicating each jolt to the dislocated knee produced the worst kind of pain. I'd bump a tree, murmur, 'Sorry' between my teeth and Uncle would whisper, 'Okay, suh, okay' and on I would stumble.

I made it to the half-hour point, Peter turning over my pack and his and hoisting Uncle onto his back for another half hour.

Carrying Uncle made climbing the peak look easy. It was 25 kilometres to go to the road head — maybe 24 now. The trail hugged a ridge, dropping off cliffs and rolling into the forest far below. The porters patted my shoulder as they passed. I picked up the double load of Peter's pack and my own and it felt like a feather after carrying Uncle. Three porters, a half hour each, and Peter to share the carrying. That gave me two hours of normal walking, then I'd be back in harness. Joe had stayed behind to photograph so he'd be safe from human porter duties, but tripods, view camera cases and videos made him look the twentieth century monster emerging from the jungle.

The trail dropped rapidly, hugging the very crest of the ridge. Spanish moss hung off the trees as the trail descended further still, the air thickened and the dry volcanic sand turned to rich earth. By early afternoon the trail dropped off a cliff; Uncle slid down like a human toboggan into a deep gorge, the trees towering overhead. At 1 p.m. lunch was a hard roll, goat cheese and a cup of tea heated in a tin on a smoking fire. My second turn under Uncle was easier, my mind ready to endure the inevitable pain but knowing I could actually walk for half an hour with a man on my back.

The day was flying along, the sun disappearing behind the cover of jungle. Wandering down a thin track in pitch black looked more and more probable. My final turn as porter for the day bent me double. Peter and I were now taking turns, the porters having fallen behind with our loads. We'd do 200 metres at a fast walk, thighs burning, then trade, sliding Uncle from one back to the other to avoid losing time picking him up or setting him down. Darkness settled, my thigh muscles were jelly, my knees grinding and my shoulders sagging further with every carry. The sun went down. A fence loomed, then a farm and finally, the park gate. We'd made it. Home, at least for a night. Kilimanjaro hovered a very long way above, again a distant peak. We pitched the tent in a cow paddock and collapsed after a warm Coke from the ranger's private stock for dinner.

The morning brought a lazy start and soon the Land Rover

arrived, chugging up the hill in a cloud of dust. The climbing equipment was buried in packs and it was back to shorts and sandshoes for the return to the tropics. Vehicular travel was a shock, once so commonplace but suddenly new and exciting. We were whisked effortlessly away and down the hill, air rushed through the windows, shouts of children by the roadside faded and passed, the mix of oil, gas and hot engine smells wafted off the Land Rover. Down and down, the endless slope of Kilimanjaro still dominated the landscape as the road passed through tropical forest and out into the fields of coffee beans. Square wooden houses sprang up, then a village, then the highway, the Land Rover accelerating to breakneck speed.

The hospital was three stories, white, with open windows swinging on squeaky hinges, a solid squat building set on the edge of Moshi. Under a tree outside, thirty people lolled in various states of disrepair in the shade, awaiting treatment. At the entrance another thirty patients stood in what looked like it might be a queue. Inside, hundreds lined the walls of the long, wide corridor, seated on a low bench running the length of the wall, with a number of people spilling onto the cement floor. It was marginally cleaner than expected, and marginally cooler.

Peter had briefed me before we arrived. 'Just stay close by me. Uncle could wait in line for months, but maybe you can help him. You are just the right colour and height to convince them.' I followed Peter dutifully from reception to office to office, ir.terspersed with half-hour waits for reasons unknown. Finally the Chief Surgeon came out and in the exact centre of the 200 waiting people, with Uncle perched on a stool, explained to me what had happened and what he proposed to do, all related in carefully enunciated English. The audience stood around in respectful silence. The doctor gave me two options, as if I knew anything about it, and I deferred to his opinion. 'Would you like it done now?' he queried. 'Immediately, if at all possible,' I said. 'Fine, we will use this room,' he said, ushering us to the end of the hall. 'Would you like to watch?'

The operating theatre, a corner room with a low window opening onto the outside parking lot, a single rickety operating table, a bare light bulb and a low table with a few scalpels, didn't inspire much confidence. Five days on Kilimanjaro hadn't prepared me for what was estimated at three hours of knee surgery, even if I'd be little more than a casual observer. 'No thank you,' I replied, but I couldn't help checking, 'Do you use anaesthetic?' 'Oh yes,' the doctor assured me with a confident smile. 'We use ether, it is very well tested.' I didn't envy Uncle Porter and said a quick prayer he lived through the ordeal. I gave Uncle's hand a squeeze as I left. 'You'll be okay.' 'Yes suh, yes suh, okay, thank you,' he murmured and gave a quick smile.

'You do not know how helpful you have been,' said Peter when we returned to the Land Rover. 'You saw all the people, some very bad, we could have waited a week. Or a month. Now he will get good treatment, we will take him home tomorrow. It is a wonderful thing. Thank you, thank you.' Jumping the queue may have been unfair, but with plans to leave the following day and feeling responsible for looking after anyone we'd hired, immediate treatment seemed the best option. I wasn't sure it was an environment where 'fair' had rules and the least we could do was help the one person we knew and respected who needed it.

Peter had obviously been uncertain whether the accident had prejudiced us against him, torn between his need to look after his uncle and fulfil his contract to us. After we'd got to know him, he'd related some of the bad yet often humorous experiences with the endless streams of tourists he'd guided up the regular route. After our five days working together, Peter was more fellow climber than employee.

The shower was cold but heavenly. The advantage of a cold shower is you don't have to worry about running out of hot water. Joe had friends-of-friends teaching at the American school in Moshi and they phoned to invite us to dinner. Their house stood alone in several acres of manicured grounds, complete with gate-keeper. The cool evening breezes wafted through wide windows, birds called from the nearby forest, sun slanted through the trees, the land rose in a single slope in the inevitable rush towards Kilimanjaro. Our hosts were Americans; he'd flown fighter jets in the Vietnam war and returned to a country as disillusioned with his war service as he soon became with the friends he'd left behind. Tanzania wasn't exactly the most common, or accessible, country to emigrate to, but that is where they had ended up. We whiled away the evening hours with conversation floating from tales of Africa to dropping bombs in North Vietnam. By midnight we'd consumed enough Tanzanian coffee to make up for the instant coffee we'd never found and wandered back down the hill to our hotel. It was a welcome change from our life in the bush, the return to African culture and the quiet confidence of our new friends.

The Land Rover packed with porters, Peter and Uncle Porter arrived after breakfast the next day. Knee surgery was $120 and we added another $200 to Uncle's funds to see him through the next couple of months of recovery. He didn't know what to say and just kept nodding appreciatively. He looked remarkably well considering what he must have gone through, his knee put back in joint and kneecap slid into place from the middle of his thigh. Just the thought made my own knees shake. Joe gave Peter a brightly coloured head-lamp to replace his temperamental flashlight on his pre-dawn starts up Kilimanjaro and we added the customary tip plus a bit more to make up his bonus. They roared off with waves and farewells in Swahili floating back in the wind.

We returned to breakfast. Kilimanjaro was over, the adventure complete. We now felt relaxed and confident in Tanzania and with Tanzanians, in no hurry to rush off. We dragged out the *Guide to Africa*. We didn't have much time, but it seemed foolish to come all this way and not see even one lion. The names of the game parks rolled romantically off the tongue, the Serengeti, Amboseli, Ngorongoro. The last was described as 'a zoo without walls'. Perfect.

Ice-encrusted rocks set along the ridge of Australia's Snowy Mountains.

ABOVE: *Aconcagua from Base Camp, the Polish Glacier the obvious swath of ice leading down and right from the summit. My only regret – I still hadn't seen a guanaco.*

BELOW: *Suspended on the Southeast Ridge, the South Face I'd ascended three years previously falling away 3,000 metres to the right.*

Self-portrait in the depths of the Messner Couloir, with the rocks just catching the morning sun, 5,000 metres up and 1,000 metres to the summit.

ABOVE: *Afternoon clouds building over Mt Foraker.*
BELOW: *At mid-height on the Messner Couloir, I stand out as a dot, lower centre, just where the couloir sweeps right.*

ABOVE: *From the slopes of Elbrus, the Caucasus Mountains cut dramatically across the boundary between Russia and Georgia.*

BELOW: *Pruitt II, crouching on the slopes of Elbrus at just under 4,000 metres, is the staging point for the summit bid. Behind the hut, silver plaques riveted to the rock commemorate those who have died or vanished on the slopes above.*

Looking up into the clouds of Elbrus's twin summits through the volcanic ridges and crevasses of the lower slopes.

ABOVE: *Living where storms blow up in an instant. Camp was set to take advantage of natural cover, sheltered in the lee of a crevasse.*

BELOW: *Ice crystals floating in filigreed lightness, every step sending them wafting like feathers.*

ABOVE: *The first ascent of Mt Atkinson, looking south from the summit at midnight, the South Pole 1,200 kilometres distant, Mt Mads the prominent peak in the right foreground.*

BELOW: *From the summit plateau at 5,000 metres on Vinson, the Ridge falling away to the left, my crampon tracks just visible in the brick-hard ice at bottom centre, points skating along the surface.*

Part of Jay Smith's party, guide Conrad Anker, with Clive Duval, Steve Plumb and Paul Teten, setting out up the unexplored glacier leading to Mt Vinson.

On a training climb for Everest below the Kangshung Face.

ABOVE: *Everest from the south, the top just visible on the left over the Nuptse Ridge with Lhotse, the world's fourth tallest peak, on the right, clouds streaming across its South Face.*

BELOW: *The world's highest altitude pack animal, the yak. Unable to live below 3,000 metres, they carry 60 kilograms all day and provide the Tibetans with wool, leather, meat and even horns to put inside their own yak bells – and they'll still hook you with a playful horn at the end of the day.*

On the Rongbuk Glacier, at the base of Everest's North Face, mushroom rock sprouts from the ice for climber Paul Teare to shelter below.

ABOVE: *The East Rongbuk glacial stream, a monsoon torrent blocking the way to Advanced Base Camp, is crossed hanging from a Tyrolean rope bridge. In the morning ice caked the ropes, ensuring a particularly quick ride, and by the end of the expedition rope stretch often doused us with a shower.*

BELOW: *Paul Teare skirting crevasses and dodging cloud shadows en route to High Camp at 6,300 metres, below Everest's North Face.*

ABOVE: *Sunset over Changtse from the North Face of Everest.*
BELOW: *Unhappy camper at 8,000 metres.*

Michael Bearzi departing high camp at 8,000 metres in the Great Couloir, North Face, Mt Everest.

CHAPTER 13

LAZY LIONS

THE BUS ROARED back down the highway to Arusha, an hour away and the gateway to Ngorongoro Crater. The hotel was mid-seventies, ten stories, balconies looking south over the rolling hills. The bar had cold Cokes and hot food. Tour groups from around the world wandered in the foyer. Polyester-clad, safari-suited Americans talked in loud voices in the coffee shop. A well-dressed woman in the dining hall pointed us to a travel agency run by the Danish Consul. In a town filled with unscrupulous operators, this seemed a safe choice. Three days, a driver, a Land Rover with the roof cut out and a view platform to stand up on were traded for $2,500. Big game viewing was obviously big business, but the price was also dictated by our desire to travel on our own and at our own speed with Joe able to photograph as he wished. Neither of us would have lasted more than a few hours on a guided bus tour. We'd also read of a spectacular old hotel set on the very rim of the Ngorongoro Crater that seemed the perfect place to celebrate the ascent of Kilimanjaro.

The black asphalt strip wound out over the brown hills, like a snake coiling over the earth. The incessant slope of Kilimanjaro was left behind, the earth rolling in all directions now that it had freed itself from Africa's tallest peak. An hour out of Arusha the Land Rover turned onto a well-travelled but rough road, with pot-holes the size of small lakes and washouts cutting away half the road in the gulches. Land Rovers with oversize tyres, industrial strength school buses and vintage Bedford trucks toiled along, tourists in newly purchased safari hats and Save the Elephant T-shirts sprouting from the windows.

By mid-afternoon the hills rolled upwards, as though we'd run up against another swell of land like Kilimanjaro. The Land Rover growled up the outside of the crater, climbing over 1,000 metres from the plain below to the rim. The green of the land intensified in patchwork plots of brighter hue, soaking in the African sun. Like nature's chequerboard, red patches of freshly tilled earth stood out in stark contrast, the farm lanes weaving through them along rickety fencelines. The temperature cooled and the road wound back and forth, finally entering the forest rimming the top of the crater. A troop of baboons popped up alongside the road, berating us from a hill, the little ones running in circles with excitement while the old ones looked on knowingly as we stared back. Who was in the zoo here, us or the animals?

We popped out on the rim, a sudden transition from the depths of the forest to an expansive view, the eye following the dip of several hundred metres into the crater, then slowly taking in the trees and hills at the base, extending into the plains and dull silver lakes in the middle, floating on across to the gentle rise on the far rim, 18 kilometres away. It was an immense and private world, an oasis the great beasts had called home for centuries. Through the binoculars, lone bull elephants could be seen wandering below; a massive herd of wildebeest grazed next to a lake speckled with pink flamingos. A small herd of zebras wandered under a tree at the base and water sloshed from a pool where the head of a hippopotamus floated just above the surface. The sun slanted in arcs through the late afternoon clouds.

The hotel was quietly elegant, formal without being stuffy, rustic but with hot water and the old fittings classic as opposed to broken. The bags were taken down the path to a line of rooms built with rough-hewn wooden walls, dark beams inset with whitewashed walls of stone and wood. The beds were large and over-stuffed, windows looked out over the creaking wooden deck and criss-crossed rail into the crater. The sun beamed off the far rim and settled in a gold ball over the plains of the Serengeti.

'Dinner at seven,' and the porter departed with a nod and a smile. We had been living in the hills, so an excuse for another shower was rarely needed, and even less excuse for an early trip to the bar. The old dark wood was set in arched beams across the ceiling ten metres overhead. Thick stone walls radiated warmth and protection in the cool evening air, the lower level a line of windows looking out over the crater. A circular stone fireplace dominated the middle of the room, separating the bar and dining areas. The bar stools were low and solid, the walls graced with pictures of the hotel's history, photos of Roosevelt on safari and Masai standing over a slain lion, the sword still dripping blood. It felt like the heart of Africa, even though it was a hotel. The white tablecloths and rows of silver were a welcome change from the days of green bananas, an English party touring the park welcome company as we traded stories and shared rounds of nightcaps into the late hours. The retreat to the room was watched by imaginary lions and wildebeests lurking in the shadows.

The alarm summoned me from the deep covers into a cold dark room. The rim of the crater was at over 2,000 metres and the air refreshingly cool, the floor freezing to the bare feet. Fortified by an English-style mixed grill breakfast and a pot of coffee, extra provisions stashed in the cooler and more coffee in the thermos, we set off in the Land Rover around the rim of the crater, the sun just tipping the edge of the horizon, melting the crater awake as light slid down into its base, like the sun being poured into an earthly bowl. Our driver, Steve, or an unpronounceable Swahili name about a metre long, was obviously happy with his work, humming Swahili songs and driving off the track to show us hidden vistas, taking up where Peter left off in kidding me about leopards leaping out of the trees lining the road and through our viewing hole. 'White boy for breakfast, their favourite,' he said with a big white-toothed smile. 'You know the big cats will start to eat you before you die if they catch you, they like the blood still hot.' This was just what I needed at dawn, dropping into lion heaven. The African sense of humour was subtle and natural, playing on day-to-day life, then twisting it gently into a laugh that seemed to pop back into the memory with a smile hours later.

The road cut abruptly off the rim and descended a thin jeep trail, a long slow curve, circling a frying pan into the fire. Through the binoculars, the tiny moving dots sprouted legs and became elephants. The roof slid back and Joe and I popped our heads out of the viewing hole, rolling along with the rhythm of the road like officers in a tank going to war. The long curve emerged into the base of the crater, inside the zoo, with us penned behind the walls of our Land Rover, the animals wandering past and viewing us at their whim. I hoped we didn't run out of petrol.

We pulled up behind another Land Rover and a woman running off behind some trees 100 metres away to relieve herself. A group of Masai warriors in traditional costume stood beside the road, spears looming over their heads. They kept one eye out to make sure no one took a photograph of them for free and another on the lady in the bushes. Steve leaned close to me and said in a low voice, 'It is the Masai's best money-earning trick. Always at this place, the ladies have had too much coffee and are too shy to go right beside the road and so run over to the trees. The Masai have lured an old lion there by bringing him food. He is usually asleep, but sometimes he wakes up and roars when the lady disturbs him. They are alone behind the tree with their pants down and a big lion stands up and roars in their face. The Masai run over and threaten the lion with their spears, rescuing the lady. That is worth a very big tip!'

We laughed together, but the lion was sleeping or gone so I viewed no rescue that day, the Masai at least as disappointed as I was. 'That lion is so old and lazy the Masai used to sit on him to have their picture taken, but the rangers made them stop it. I don't even think he has any teeth.

'Don't worry, I'll show you some real lions, the lionesses, the ladies who do the hunting. We won't be getting out of the Land Rover then. Even the Masai don't go near them.'

Faint trails meandered through the bush. It was only 18 kilometres from one side of the crater to the other, but looked far further. The rim rose up in a perfect circle, suspended in a big bowl hung from the sky. The sun was moving rapidly above the horizon, clear and bright, the occasional cloud just beginning to form.

We drove off down the trail, disturbing a herd of zebras walking unconcerned across the road. The little ones frolicked between their mothers' legs, peeking out at us. Their bodies were square and taut, their manes and tails like leather straps. A zebra is the easiest thing in the world to focus a camera on, the stripes coming together like a focusing screen. Further down a shallow gully we came out on a plain cut by a shallow lake. Hundreds of pink flamingos stood in the pool, necks arcing into the water and then up into the sky to look around. The still water formed a perfect reflection, a flock standing upright and another below, as if they walked in tandem with a twin connected below their feet.

A herd of wildebeest moved towards the water, several thousand moving like a wave. They were aptly named, looking wilder and wilder the closer they came. Their symmetric horns and big ears framed a heavily bearded face with trails of hair grown long on their stomachs, like giant carpet sweepers. Their eyes rolled continually, as if they weren't quite sure what to do next. It was easy to see why they all stampeded at once, moving in huge migratory waves. It was probably the only way they could ever decide which direction to go. We kept our distance, Steve not wanting us to be the cause of a misplaced migration.

The hippo pond was full to the brim, hippos on top of hippos, lined up in even rows, the babies tucked in close to their mothers. They rose and fell like balloons in the water. In the zoo they always looked unhappy, moving slowly around small green and stinky pools. Here they appeared truly content, the ears twitching, their eyes bright, pushing and shoving gently against each other like a big happy family. They'd have to be pretty happy together, the pool was huge and most of them chose to crowd together in the centre in hippo heaven.

The warthogs were a mixture of a cute animal with a sideways walk, glancing over their hairy shoulders as they trotted along in the bush, and devious monsters, their tusks protruding menacingly in a moon-like curve above their lips. Skulking behind the bushes and wandering amongst the herds of wildebeest and zebra were the laughing hyenas, smiling broadly at everything, revealing a vicious set of teeth. Thin shoulders swept back to wide haunches, as if they'd been building up their hindquarters with weight training. Their sandy colour tinged with streaks of black made them nearly invisible, only their pointed ears standing up like perfect oversized triangles to mark their positions.

It wasn't only the zoo without walls, but the animals moving amongst one another, the wildebeests grazing with the zebras, the hyenas skulking between them, the pink flamingos feeding in their watering hole when they came to the pond in the evening, that created a sense of balance, of animal and nature working together.

The lions remained reclusive until the end of the day, one finally appearing lying on a low hill of grass. Watching it, Steve lightly tapped my shoulder and I turned to see another one 10 metres away padding towards us. Her head was down and the muscles rippled across her shoulders. For some reason, I'd almost expected the arrival of a lion to be heralded by trumpets and a fanfare. Having one suddenly creep up behind us, I realised how easy it would be to go from feeling completely complacent to having a lion at your neck, without hearing a sound. I would not have wanted to be a baby wildebeest right then. 'She is only curious,' said Steve, 'we are quite safe.' The feeling of silent control emanated from the lioness with frightening power.

The sun dipped along the crater rim and the Land Rover rumbled through the trees leading to the trail out the far side of the crater. The trees sheltered a mammoth bull elephant that ambled towards us. Looking at him from the top of the Land Rover, he was still taller, his tusks jutting metres in front of him. We sat silently as he approached, until Steve suddenly started the engine and revved it loudly. 'They don't like the noise,' he said. 'If they decide to, it is little work for them to tip the Land Rover over.' The elephant was so close I could look him right in the eye. And it wasn't the sleepy, 'Feed me some peanuts' look that elephants in the circus or zoo give you. This elephant was angry; we were on his trail to dinner, where he would consume 100 kilograms of fronds from the nearby gully. Steve revved the Land Rover and put it in rapid reverse, sensing the same. 'I think he is hungrier and bigger than us.'

The trail out of the crater led up a thin track, edging around the side of the steep slope leading back to the forest at the rim. The crater opened up below, revealing the herds returning from their evening wander to the watering hole, the carnivores moving out on the evening hunt, the shadows shooting across the rolling plains. It was a climb out of a day of natural magic. Over the horizon to the east, the afternoon mists were clearing on Kilimanjaro, the rising clouds tinged orange and red, filling the sky with colour.

IV
NORTH AMERICA

CHAPTER 14

KATHMANDU, DELHI, LONDON, ANCHORAGE, TALKEETNA

MCKINLEY IS A MYTHICAL white mountain tucked away in the Arctic, covered with ice and snow and surrounded by polar bears. Stories had filtered down over the years of climbers crashing through into immense crevasses, avalanches sweeping over camps, toes freezing off and grizzly bears chasing down those who chose to brave the forests surrounding the peak. A .44 Magnum pistol seemed as important a piece of equipment as an ice axe when climbing in Alaska.

Returning from an Everest expedition that had been sandwiched between Kilimanjaro and McKinley, my approach to North America started in Kathmandu, flying out as the monsoon moved in, red Tibetan dust still coating the duffles, dropping in and out of Delhi and London en route to Anchorage, Alaska. My Alaskan host, Bill Hammel, who I'd first met when he'd been our Everest doctor several years previously, was away. But his car, a black turbocharged Saab, waited in the airport parking lot. I roared off with confidence, but was still in English drive mode, and after wondering why all the street signs faced the wrong way, discovered I'd travelled halfway to Bill's house on the wrong side of the road.

Everything in Alaska was larger than life. Pine trees towered over the road and the forest stretched away over hills and up into the distant snow-capped peaks that rose up into the sky on the horizon. Roads were wide, houses big, trucks had tyres as tall as a car with treads so thick a cat could be run over and still live to see another day. The shopping centre was a warehouse with shopping buggies the size of large wheelbarrows. For the enthusiastic, pallets with forklifts could be loaded high with enough provisions for a family of eight to spend a winter in the bush.

Joe finally flew in following delays in New York, arriving three days later than planned. Duffles were packed with cheese and crackers, pasta, potatoes, carrots and a pack of reindeer sausage and we were up at dawn a day later for the train ride north to Talkeetna. After braving Swahili, green bananas and ancient Land Rovers, the comforts of 'Made in the USA' travel plans seemed almost too easy. The other peaks had been a battle just to get to; reaching McKinley was a holiday in comparison. The train attendant, in crisp blue uniform with brown hair, brown eyes and a big smile, showed us to our deep dish seats and the train chugged off as scheduled, black and potent coffee arriving within minutes of our request. Part of the Alaska tourist trail to the north, the railroad wove out of Anchorage and into the deep blue green of the forest. The engine blew smoke up through the trees far ahead of our coach, the rhythm of the rails swayed the carriages gently back and forth, the conductor pointed out moose hidden in the swamps and bears as they scurried off the tracks, while the chef prepared the salmon steaks for lunch. Maintaining a North American theme, the wine was from California and the dessert apple pie. McKinley loomed somewhere ahead, but in the meantime, little suffering was being done in the pursuit of the top of North America. In foreign lands, travel is often so frustrating that reaching the mountains and solitude was a welcome relief. Alaska proved a home away from home, as we wandered comfortably towards the heights through a huge land of creature comforts.

The train clanked to a stop in Talkeetna. Wooden cabins with pine tree gardens, four-wheel-drive pick-up trucks with rifle racks in the back windows and tall men with dark beards and thick-soled boots lined the main street. Gunfights at high noon seemed likely.

A day later we rode through the thick forest to the airport, where planes were lined up in long rows like cars in a parking lot. Cliff

Hudson, one of the original bush pilots, casually checked us in, weighing luggage and covering our ice axe and crampon points so they wouldn't put any holes in the fuselage. Skippy, his little white poodle, jumped on board as co-pilot. We bumped down the runway in that disconcerting way small planes have, like being in a Volkswagen with over-inflated tyres, until Cliff slid back the stick and the plane hopped into the air, popped out over the trees and sailed away over the forest. It was easy to see why Alaskans have so many small planes, as the immensity of the land immediately opened up when we cleared the trees. The one road rapidly disappeared and the sky was the gateway to the wilderness.

McKinley was little more than a cloudy hummock in the distance as the plane skimmed over the trees. 'That's the cabin down there where the lady called me from on her radio when the bear trapped them inside,' Cliff commented, dipping the wings so we could peer down into the lake. 'I dropped into the lake with the floats on, kept my rifle at the ready, and her and the kids came running and were straight into the plane before I even saw that bear.' Cliff related it like a commuter might tell of seeing a crash on the motorway on the way to work, a simple matter-of-fact tale, only marginally more interesting than anything else that happened during a work week.

The stories continued in a quiet drawl as we hummed towards the mountain, the nose of the plane in the air, propeller whirling steadily as the altimeter climbed, the forest thinned, the air cooled, the clouds built and the river changed from rushing water to froth, then to ice as it flowed out from underneath the glacier. The ridges rose up in waves, rock building to snow, like knife blades set jutting out from the earth. The tops were jagged and black, ice sculpted off from any level perch, like ice umbrellas hugging the ridge tops. The final wave rose up far above the rest and Cliff nosed the plane into position, shooting through a notch in the ridge, the well-named 'One Shot' because that is all you get at it. With the clouds weighing down heavily from above and the ridge rising abruptly on both sides, 'One Shot' was like threading a needle with nowhere to go but straight through into the mountains beyond.

We shot through into a land of snaking glaciers and cascading icefalls far below the plane, as the green of the forests and blue of the rivers disappeared in a sudden transition from earth to ice. The plane swung in a slow circle and the flags of the glacial airstrip appeared on a branch of the Kahiltna Glacier. The plane lined up, dipped towards the snow and dropped onto the ice in a long controlled swoop. 'Out you boys go, now, have a good time. Just give me a ring when you want to come home,' and Cliff had unloaded the duffles, skis and sleds, put two people on board and was roaring back to Talkeetna before the cloud level changed. Skippy the poodle co-pilot, who'd spent the ground time perched on the plane's tail flaps out of the snow, looked out the back of the cockpit with a sympathetic gaze as our last dose of civilised pleasure hummed out of sight. Low clouds filled the sky above and McKinley was nowhere in sight. But 100 metres away at the edge of the glacier, cliffs rose in a cascade of ice and black rock into the cloud, heralding real mountains hovering overhead.

CHAPTER 15

THE ONLY GOOD SLED IS A DEAD SLED

AT 2 A.M. A SUBTLE haze filled the air, but it was nowhere near dark. June in Alaska, a few hundred kilometres south of the Arctic Circle, was a land of perpetual light. In my sleep, voices wandered by until I went outside later myself and realised they hadn't been in my imagination at all. At the low elevation of 2,100 metres, climbers moved at night on the glaciers, when the crevasse bridges were (hopefully) frozen hard and less likely to dump them in the millions of crevasses. A few new tents sprouted out of the gloom, set in holes cut deep in the snow to protect them from wind blasts. It looked like a setting for a space-age movie, figures moving slowly, swathed in clothing, sleds in tow, candles glowing from inside the tents in our tiny civilisation.

The comforts of Alaska had suddenly disappeared. From motels, restaurants and cars we'd moved in an hour and a half to a tent, cooking over a one-burner gas stove and towing our possessions in a sled. More dramatic was the landscape. Grey snow, ice and clouds cut by black cliffs shooting up into the whiteness as tendrils of fog floated past was the welcome to our new world. There was no colour, the wind was hushed by mist, the air was thin and frosty and the ice devoid of smell. Outside the tents climbers told stories by day, waiting impatiently for flights out, and dozed in the dusk of night. The lateness of the season, dictated by my earlier Everest expedition, meant most climbers were departing just as we arrived. We'd enjoy warmer temperatures but be faced with more crevasses that would be opening by the day as summer advanced. By the second day our schedule had flip-flopped and breakfast was at 9 p.m., trading day for night for our five-day walk to Base Camp.

The approach route lay down to the bottom of the small glacier we'd landed on, followed by a very long slog up the main Kahiltna Glacier for several days, a hard right turn up and around a few smaller glaciers and into Base Camp at 4,200 metres. It wasn't something to think about in its entirety, the prospect of towing 50 kilograms up a gradual slope for nearly a week taking any hint of enthusiasm right out of the journey. But McKinley towered at the end of the slog, and if McKinley was the goal, slogging was necessary. Perhaps the scenic wonders would counteract the lack of enthusiasm, but getting overjoyed was out of the question, the crevasses would see to that.

McKinley's crevasses are infamous. All year the glaciers creep downhill, forming crevasses at every ripple and ridge they run over. The immense size of the glaciers translates into the size of the crevasses, with crater-like holes ten metres wide disappearing out of sight below into inky ice blue depths which criss-cross the glaciers everywhere. Flying in over them, it almost looked like there were more crevasses than solid ice in the glaciers, the surface swept into wave after wave of cascading ice. All winter it snows, covering the crevasses with a frosting that makes them nearly invisible. But one or ten or 30 metres down there is always a hole. Depending on snow density, temperature, wind and snow loading, crossing them can be uneventful or very interesting. Experience helps, but some of the most experienced climbers have still died on McKinley. Other climbers have just managed to live through adventures that frighten everyone else.

The climbing season extends from late April when it first warms up enough to climb, until early July when the crevasses open up to such an extent that travelling the glaciers is nearly impossible. The season had already proved the most deadly on record with the combination of crevasses, avalanches and bad storms killing eleven people. Tom Brokaw at NBC News in New York was interested in a news feature on the events surrounding the deaths, so even if traversing the crevasses as we marched up the hill felt innocuous, our interviews with rangers and rescue personnel ensured we had an ongoing commentary about the hidden dangers on McKinley. We didn't have to go looking far for stories when the second day at the airstrip a man crawled into camp from neighbouring Mt Foraker. Their team of three had nearly completed the lightly named but deadly serious Pink Panther route when an avalanche swept one teammate away and battered the other to death at the end of a rope. Colby Coombes managed to save part of a rope and spent the next two days sliding down the peak, battling a dislocated shoulder and sprained ankle, to finally reach the heavily crevassed glacier, creeping across it for days before crawling back to the airstrip.

Despite years of climbing, most of my experience in North America had been as a rock climber, ascending the alpine cliffs on the Diamond in Colorado and the big granite walls of Half Dome and El Capitan in Yosemite, California. Towing a sled up a glacier was new and novel and when friends Jim Williams and Sandy Pittman, who we'd met previously on Aconcagua, pulled into camp after their recent ascent, Joe and I humbly went for lessons. The maze of ropes required to travel safely on the glaciers without disappearing into a hole forever was like travelling with a bowl of spaghetti dumped over our heads. The basics — you coil ten metres of rope and throw it over your shoulder, you tie in with a figure eight on a big carabineer that leads to your partner, you tie a figure eight loop in front of that and clip that into a second carabineer. Then the sled is tied into a harness around your waist (over the harness that the rope is clipped into, otherwise you fall in a hole and you are strangled by your sled), and the sled is also clipped into the rope leading back to your partner (otherwise you fall in a hole and just when you thank the Lord you haven't died, the sled falls in and hits you on the head), which you must do with a sliding prussik knot (otherwise it freezes up and no matter what you do ices over and you perish because you can't adjust the knot once the sled falls in a crevasse even though you haven't). As I said, these are the basics, though other things may go wrong. It is important to add that you don't just wear the skis, they must also be tied to your waist harness with short lengths of cord. This allows you to fall in a crevasse, release your bindings (assuming you can reach them), not lose your skis (assuming they haven't been broken already) and then ascend the rope on your sliding prussik knots (assuming they are not iced over) and climb out of the crevasse to safety, still with your skis, which were supposed to keep you from falling in the crevasse in the first place. These lessons taught me two irrevocable rules.

1. Never fall in a crevasse
2. If you fall in a crevasse, pray you die quickly.

At two in the morning, with five days of glacial travel ahead, this seemed like a late date for a sled lesson. But the peak beckoned and there was no real excuse not to start in its direction. With all the mental power required to keep the ropes straight, the first step was still worse than expected. A sled doesn't slide or slip, except in a direction contrary to the direction you'd like it to travel. As we slid away from the airstrip and out onto the great expanse of the glacier we were encouraged by Sandy Pittman. 'Most expeditions fail between here and the toilet. If you can just make it past there you'll be fine.' With the toilet little more than 50 metres outside of camp, it didn't take us long to increase the odds of success. Then my sled slid past me on a downhill section and began dragging me down the hill instead of the other way around, my skis gained speed, Joe yelled from behind and tumbled into a heap, the rope brought me to an abrupt halt, the sled rope nearly sliced me in half, cutting into my stomach, and my skis twisted sideways and fell off. I'd thought there may be an art to sled travel, a skill to be mastered. But over the next five days of slogging, I came to only one conclusion: the only good sled is a dead sled.

At the base of the small glacier where the plane had landed, the route turned right and opened into the grand expanse of the Kahiltna Glacier. In the midnight gloom it was a grey field of rolling snow hiding endless crevasses, the snow rising in ever bigger mounds for kilometres and kilometres. Mt Foraker towered along-side, an immense mass that was still 1,000 metres lower than McKinley. Imagining anything bigger was frightening. The gloom turned to fog, the swish of the skis and skins was a whisper against the snow. Peering into the murk, we found the snow blended with the mist. The only distinguishing features were our ski tips, sluicing forward, marking the dips and rises in the snow. The skis floated like a boat on a hidden swell, rising and falling with no perceptible change in slope. Hours marched on, snow began to fall and by morning it was time for bed. The tent was unpacked in a hollow, the stove roared, hot chocolate was served, potatoes and tomatoes were sliced fresh into the stew, the frost melting off with a sizzle as they fell into the pot.

By nightfall, which was daytime in sled time, colour was still absent from the great outdoors. The skis were again pointed uphill, the ropes all laid out in a line, snaking through the snow, dipping over the crevasse bridges, some so wide that if they had collapsed we'd have both dropped in. By midnight the storm started and the snow fell like night. Visibility was down to the tips of the skis. The glacier grew steeper to the point where pitching the tent would be far more work than pleasure, digging out a platform. An occasional bamboo pole popped into sight, denoting the way ahead. From their flared tips flags sprouted, like prayer flags waving in the wind in Tibet. Old abandoned tent sites with tent walls frozen and sculpted in the wind and tunnels bored through them by the sun appeared from the mist, like the strange Tibetan mud forts, the dzongs that I'd just left behind in the retreat from Everest. In the cloud, direction was maintained only by keeping the skis flat against the hill, a slide onto the edges indicating a turn from the endlessly rising slope. The murk finally yielded a shadowed tent hole that required only minimal excavation, the tent was pitched a few minutes later and the pasta was bubbling away, an extra chilli and two extra bay leaves thrown in to ward off the storm. The day grew darker and four hours later I was up again, into layers of clothing, digging out the tent walls to save them from collapsing; an hour was spent shovelling endless white fluff in the half-grey light of another Arctic night. Getting to McKinley was turning into a battle.

The lower glaciers on McKinley are often covered in clouds and storm, so staying put wasn't an option if we wanted to reach the mountain. It felt more and more like we were living in a huge white cave. Outside stimulus faded. Snow fell, clouds covered the peaks and the gentle roll of the glacier formed our world. The feeling of Arctic expanse had disappeared altogether.

That night we awoke to snow coloured grey with ash. It melted in the pan to leave a fine black sand. Not until we met descending climbers a day later did we learn a volcano had blown up 150 kilometres away and the resulting blast had spread ash over the mountains like a layer of black snow. Above the tent, it stood out on the peaks in high contrast; fresh avalanche paths showed as streaks of white while the lee side of ridges where the wind slowed held drifts of black snow. If the white environment had been surreal to start with, it now became even more so with the advent of the black snowstorm. Blown by the wind, the grey cast on the snow wasn't consistent. Dark streaks marked indentations in the snow while the ridges were blown clean and white. The volcano had swept the clouds from the area and the sky set its deep blue shadow above the mountains as the route wound up the hill to the head of the Kahiltna Glacier.

At 3,000 metres the glacier finally climbed out of the low-level cloud and emerged into the heights of the peaks. Like popping out from beneath the clouds on a plane flight, the transition was immediate, moving from snow-cave reality to an expanse of mountains above and below that rolled and stretched away over the horizon as if they went on forever. A hard right turn took us to the base of Motorcycle Hill. A steep climb led up and around the base of the West Buttress and onto Base Camp. It was hard to tell whether Motorcycle Hill was so named because it was too steep for a motorcycle, or not steep enough; whether a motorcycle had been ridden up, or down it, or if someone just wished they had one to ride.

While my original plan had been to ascend the classic Cassin Ridge route on McKinley's south side, Joe's delayed departure from New York had necessitated a change of route to make our approach less complicated and speed up the ascent. By following the approach to the traditional West Buttress route, glacial travel had been relatively straightforward and we'd pop out onto a plateau where we could put Base Camp at just over 4,000 metres. From there, the face rose in a clean sweep of 1,800 metres to the summit ridge. In photographs it looked ideal for a solo, the face starting close to Camp so I wouldn't have to travel through any extensive crevasses, always the worst fear of the soloist. At the summit ridge I would link up with the West Buttress route, providing an easy descent, dropping me back into camp down a route followed by many climbers.

The route that stood out on the broad face was the Messner Couloir. Certain climbers have a penchant for climbing mountains in certain ways, depending on their abilities and styles. I'd discovered that Messner often had an eye for the direct approach, utilising natural lines that combined the best climbing and the fastest route to the summit, ideal for a soloist. But looking at a photograph of a 1,800-metre face and actually standing beneath it could elicit far different feelings, so I resolved to wait until I had the opportunity to view the route at first hand before making the final decision to ascend it.

At the base of Motorcycle Hill, a mound of snow piled high was a home for the skis, as the route above was too steep for them to be of use. If pulling the sleds up the glacier below had proved difficult, ascending a forty-degree slope dragging what felt like a huge dead pig through the drifted snow was murder. Hidden crevasses still sprouted from the slope in places no crevasse should be. Halfway up, one leg disappeared to mid-thigh to reveal a hole curving off in a wave of icy blue. Down the glacier, a lone helicopter, looking mosquito-like against the huge backdrop of Mt Foraker, circled the slopes searching for the bodies of the two climbers left behind. The sun shone yellow and bright above, the clouds wafted peaceably up the Kahiltna Glacier and I remembered the words of a fellow climber on one of my first rescues above Boulder, Colorado, 'What a beautiful day to die.' The weather could be perfect and spirits high, but it often was just before everything changed. The magnificence of McKinley could easily lull climbers into a feeling of complacency, the biggest danger.

The sleds slid around Windy Corner as if on sails, the mountain opening up behind the ridge onto a huge plateau cut by a final crevasse big enough to hold a small village. To the left, the West Buttress route swept up a series of fixed ropes onto a spectacular ridge. Directly ahead, the face loomed, far larger than any photograph. It dominated the skyline, rising up and up until it seemed a part of the sky. The Messner Couloir shot up through the right side of the cliffs, simple and direct, just a lot bigger in reality than it seemed it should be.

Base Camp was a series of tent holes set in the snow, ice blocks built up around the outside. The season's storms had raised the snow walls higher and higher until just the tops of the tents poked out, flashes of colour above the white plain. With up to fifty people in residence at a time, it looked like an Eskimo village, with even the occasional igloo sprouting from the snow. As the season was closing down, only a few climbers wandered about, tent sites were pre-dug and it was like moving into a suburban neighbourhood on the wrong side of town with vacancies everywhere. At the Rangers' camp, manned during the high season, the walls were coming down, trunks stacked with the season's provisions loaded for the helicopter lift out a day later.

Daryl Miller, a ranger who had spent the season at the camp, had stories that could have filled two books. With the experience of a man who had seen one mountaineering disaster after another, he still maintained a laconic sense of humour about climbers' failings. 'The Koreans left camp during a lull in the storm, reached that nice level patch just up the hill when it started to storm again and so they decided to camp.' Daryl waved his arm at the hill, where the only flat spot I could see, even from 300 metres below, was the bridge of an immense crevasse that cut the slope. 'Yes, that's it,' Daryl said, 'right in the middle of the crevasse. Well of course it fell in and they all ended up down the hole. One of them made it out and down to us. We crawled up the hill in the middle of the storm and the middle of the night, lowered 25 metres down into the crevasse and dug one man out who had been impaled upside down in soft snow and couldn't move. Must have been there for three hours by the time we reached him. He had some pretty bad back and neck problems but, after a visit to the Anchorage hospital, is probably home now.'

'Has anyone been up the Messner Couloir lately?' I asked, looking for information about my proposed route.

'Not up,' said Daryl, 'but down. Four Canadians were on the summit ridge, on the way back from the top. They were all roped together and ran into clouds and a storm. I was watching from here and could see them moving in and out of the clouds. They were way off route, around those rock cliffs, when one of them slipped, pulling the others off. They didn't stop until they had fallen all the way through the hourglass to below those rock cliffs at the bottom.'

'Are they still there?' I asked. The last thing I wanted to do was have to climb over four dead climbers on my start up McKinley.

'No, we managed to pull them out by helicopter a while ago. There might be a few things that got torn off them, but I'd say the route is pretty clear. I haven't heard of anybody doing it in a few years, though.'

I didn't ask, but hoped that whatever Daryl referred to being torn off didn't include any arms or legs. A pack or hat I didn't mind, but climbing falls weren't known for being gentle. The one avalanche I'd been dragged through on Everest had left me feeling as if I'd been on the rack and my first reaction had been to check to see if my arms and legs were still all attached. The route didn't actually look that steep, but if the Canadians had fallen the entire distance, it was a good indication that any slip would land me in the same place.

110

Overnight, the drama faded and by the next morning the reality of the Messner Couloir, broken down into sections through the binoculars, looked very straightforward, a clean simple line straight up the Couloir to the ridge, a right turn, a short walk over the Football Field and 100 metres to the summit, followed by a dash down the West Buttress. Mapping the route in the mind was always an essential prerequisite, feeling the body already on the route, anticipating timing and difficulties, thinking through the obstacles. Then I borrowed a book and disappeared into the world of dinosaurs, wandering through Jurassic Park, leaving the mountain and my climbing mind alone for a day. The physical difficulties of the face I felt comfortable with, but the sheer size of the mountain was intimidating. Once all the background work had been done, the route scouted, the decisions made on equipment and timings calculated, the best thing to do was let instinct take over. Being born a climber, all I had to do now was let my intuition play its part.

CHAPTER 16

THE MESSNER COULOIR

With the disappearance of day and night in the Arctic, starting the climb at a given hour made little difference. Slightly lower temperatures during the dusk from midnight to 3 a.m. needed to be avoided at the top, but the starlight starts of South America and Africa could be avoided. At 7 a.m. my body was still in full retreat in a shell of self-preservation. Waking up was slow, crackers induced nausea, coffee tasted bitter, bootlaces ended up tied together and the only motivation was to return to the warmth of the sleeping bag and cover my head.

The sun soon crept through the doorway, inspiring life. A litre of water, a thermos of coffee, a peanut butter and jam sandwich and a light down jacket went into the waist pack. McKinley appeared to be leaning over to squash me, the mountain huge overhead, my resources and resolve dwarfed. How many footsteps in 1,800 metres of climbing, how many chances to slip, just once, and slide straight back down again? The ice axe gave me something to grasp, the reassuring swing of the pick cutting through the air. I started out over the snow plain to the base of the face, while behind me a few climbers toiled off in the opposite direction towards the West Buttress, carrying packs reaching high over their heads to stock their next camp. Most would spend a day getting onto the ridge 600 metres higher, another day moving up to a High Camp at 5,100 metres, a rest day somewhere in between, a final day to the summit and then a day retreating back to Base Camp, as long as all went to schedule and bad weather didn't cause any delays. My own sack lunch and extra jacket seemed a little absurd, like a schoolkid setting off for the first day of school. I counteracted my feelings of inadequacy by facing the mountain, peering upwards as the angle of the climb changed, watching how the light altered over the ice cliffs, how shadows fell on the snow high on the face, all signals of snow density, steepness and where to climb.

From the camp the face looked like one big snow slope, but every move closer changed perspective and held clues on the best route, how to avoid the soft snow and skirt the rocks that lurked just below the surface and would slow climbing up higher. From the middle of a big face, it is very hard to tell where you are. Little can be seen and if the climb isn't mapped in memory before starting and anything goes wrong, you don't know what to do or where to go. If the face avalanched in the sun, the cliffs started dropping rocks in my path or the seemingly gentle snow ramp exit was actually black ice, it would be too late and I'd have to retreat or face wasting time climbing around the obstacle. What this face lacked in difficulty it made up for in size, magnifying even a small mistake a thousand times.

The climbing rhythm built as camp faded, leaving safety below to become a part of the mountain. There was the familiar crunch of crampons into the snow and the ice axe pulled me forward. The couloir grew quickly steeper, crevasses faded to be replaced by bergschrunds, ice walls built up around the cliffs at the base of the face. The route spidered through them, then crept into the base of the couloir, a clean sweep running straight up through the hourglass of rock, into the summit snowfield and through the cliffs below the ridge. As I looked down, Camp was already a small dot of tents, the morning clouds building on the glacier below, floating up from the lowlands like a mist on the white rivers of snow.

For the first time I could look out over the surrounding ridges and across Alaska. The glaciers crept into the forest with fingers of ice running into the black of the rivers. Lakes spotted the green expanse and black pools reflected the clouds. Further out a sea of dark, almost black, green forest flowed endlessly south and slid out of sight into the Bering Sea. Unlike Aconcagua or Kilimanjaro, whose routes had wound and twisted upwards, the single sweep of the face made me feel smaller and smaller. From below, where the rock cliffs pinched together in the steepest part of the route to form a distinct hourglass, the snow had looked a mere icicle. Climbing through the icicle, it was 50 metres wide, the snow turning to hard névé, crisp and fast under the crampons. Speed was balanced against the need for every point to be set straight into the snow, the front points of the crampons biting with a distinct squeak, ice axe points swung and sunk to the hilt. The climbing wasn't steep enough to be difficult, but step after step had to be perfect, the aura of the Canadians tumbling by still reflecting from the confines of the couloir.

By noon the sun had crept around the ridge and was shadowing my footsteps. My trail left the hourglass and meandered upwards past rocks sprouting like toadstools from the cliffs. At 1 p.m. a mushroom of rock was swept clear to form a picnic table, legs straddling the hump like riding a saddle of ice, the heels of crampons hitched up high to ward off slippage into the void ahead. The view had changed from looking down a mountain to looking out a plane window, the top of Mt Foraker just below, the Kahiltna Glacier set kilometres distant in a cloud and weather system separate from the mountain. The coffee was still hot but the peanut butter and jam was frozen solid. I broke it into ice-cube-sized bites and melted it with coffee slurps. The climb was like back to back marathons, pushing gently but never to excess, the reserve to finish more important than current speed. Still, the mountain was falling away quickly and the cliffs that marked the ridge above slid perceptibly closer. Lunch was finished, though raspberry seeds still stuck between my teeth, and the track wove upwards, through ankle- and then knee-deep snow.

'Screech.' The hidden, deadly McKinley surfaced below the ridge, crampons skittering on black ice, like fingernails on a blackboard. Muscles tensed, relaxed. I curved right, up, left, another patch, impenetrable, weaving now, so close to the ridge. The only way out was a long traverse, then straight up into the broken cliffs to avoid the ice. Above the rocks the angle changed from danger back to safety so fast I stepped straight off the top of the face and sat down. The reason for the Canadians' fall was now clear, the black ice, the fatigue and being lost in the clouds above the couloir all combined into a single slip on the hidden ice that pulled them all to their deaths. McKinley moved from benign to deadly and back again in an instant, a chameleon whose ice had changed from friendly white to deadly black in a step.

Clouds built on the glaciers rushed up the peak and whirled about in an afternoon storm. The route led out onto the Football Field, a huge flat expanse. Leaving the confines of the face, the world spread out to the east, north and west, the ridges of McKinley stretching away, dropping into the glaciers and the forest. To the north the light was deep blue, as if the world grew colder and colder, the polar bears of my childhood wandering on the ice just over the horizon. Having rejoined the popular West Buttress route, I expected to meet other climbers, but the mountain was empty, seemingly devoid of life. I slipped into my extra jacket and crept up the final hill. A track of footprints a few centimetres wide led along the final ridge, a snow crest suspended above the South Face. On the right it dropped 3,000 metres to the glacier below, on the left it swept steeply down to the northern glacier. I wandered up it, suspended on the ridge, clouds rising around me, clambering over cornices and ice mushrooms. Abruptly the ridge dropped away towards the far side of the mountain and I stopped. There was nothing above me, but having concentrated totally on the climb and going up, stopping at the top was an abrupt conclusion, a physical reality that left the rest of me still ready to climb higher.

Cloud whirled about but the wind was low, gusting briefly then fading completely. I finished the peanut butter and jam sandwich and the coffee. North America spread out at my feet, the spectacular summit ridge a curl of cornices overhanging the South Face by ten metres, like ice diving boards extending into space. Through my wide-angle 16 mm lens, my shadow floated on the snow of the summit and the Arctic Circle hovered in the background. Colours were snow-white and dark forest, a peculiar density of blue-black with a purple tinge on the edges. I sat for nearly two hours as the rising mists faded and cleared, peaks rose out of the clouds far below and the glaciers snaked off into the dark forests. The sun was still high in the sky, my 5 p.m. arrival still enjoying the heat that was late midday in the far north. Thoughts of success never surfaced, the top being only a geographical point on the climb. There would be plenty of time for euphoria and celebrations later. Crevasses would be as easy to fall into on the way down as the way up and fatigue would make the ice even more dangerous. My summit thoughts turned directly from the ascent to the challenge of the descent, without pause for congratulations.

The traditional West Buttress route was far less steep than the Messner Couloir and would provide a rapid descent back to camp. I also wanted to experience the route, one of the classic climbs in North America that I had always heard so much about. It rolled off the summit ridge, back across the Football Field, then arced right along a subsidiary ridge, dropping along the top of one of the immense glaciers weaving their way down McKinley's northern slopes. If the southern side of the mountain had felt big, the northern side had a completely different feel, the glacier rolling out from between the north and south summits, already a mighty river of ice fed from the top of North America.

The slopes were gentler but wider, rolling downhill in long waves, sliding into rivers and on into the hazy depths of the forest another world away below. Off the precipitous heights of the south side, following the crampon scratchings of the West Buttress climbers, my legs flew along, as if on a highway home. As the air thickened, fatigue faded. The High Camp at 5,100 metres soon popped into view, but I wandered through during dinner hour with few climbers in view. The sun slanted orange towards a sunset, still hours away, light rays outlining the ridge and the red rocks along its crest. The light glowed through layers of atmosphere on the horizon, the sky strewn with a palette of colours weeping from the sun. Still the legs ran on, rushing past ropes fixed in the snow for heavily laden parties, past a lone platform of a party who'd stopped to camp along the way, dropping finally to the low point on the ridge, a crest with a slide west or east to exit. The track led east, a dual line of ropes lying on the snow, for uphill and downhill traffic, like a Disneyland rollercoaster track. Looking far out across the face I saw a tiny line of tracks etched into the Messner Couloir, marking my route. Two hours after leaving the summit, I wandered back into Base Camp from the top of North America.

CHAPTER 17

NORTH AMERICA TIMES TWO

'HEY, THIS LOOKS INCREDIBLE, is this really what it looks like?' Joe was playing back the video footage from the summit ridge. I'd walked along the knife-edged ridge with the camera held at waist height in one hand and my ice axe gripped firmly in the other. Just looking through the small viewfinder on the video inspired vertigo, the skinny trail of ice set along the classic knife-edge ridge. 'I'd really like to climb McKinley you know, Robert, I think it is the most important of the peaks to me.' I lay half asleep. It was the fourth of July, America's and Joe's birthday. Having climbed McKinley the day before, another ascent held little interest, but Joe wanted to go to the top. 'And we could use more footage for NBC, Robert,' added Joe.

At 7 a.m. the next morning, Joe started plying me with coffee, a turbocharged blend that three cups and an overflowing bowl of porridge later sent us on the trail upwards. Having just descended the West Buttress, I had the route well rehearsed. Plans had been carefully laid. Not wanting to camp, we'd have to ascend and re-turn in a day. I'd carry the pack, food, extra clothes, stove and video; Joe would be limited to one camera only, a sacrifice rare in the extreme.

Four hours out of Base Camp we reached the High Camp, cached the stove and headed for the top. Ten hours later we came out on the summit ridge and Joe had his real-life view of the top of North America. But the hour was late and cold; ice-laden winds had replaced the semi-tropical temperatures I'd enjoyed two days previously. After fifteen minutes on top we descended back into the gloom of an Arctic night, returning to the tent six hours later. The next day, following two journeys to the top of McKinley in three days, was truly a rest day, the sun heating the tent to sauna temperature by noon. But with the crevasses opening by the day, there was no excuse to wait for any more holes to form and, following a late lunch, we were on the downward trail, curving around a curiously quiet windy corner, sliding down Motorcycle Hill and into the camp where our skis rested, melted into the snow wall.

The next night, skis pointed downhill, we slid out onto the expanse of the Kahiltna Glacier, opening up the throttle on the downhill run. Ropes tangled, sleds slewed sideways, crevasses appeared out of the dusk like pre-dug graves. The crevasses were splitting between descending parties. Ski tracks led over a bridge that an hour later had disappeared, revealing a five-metre gap disappearing into the ice. Joe came to a sudden halt at the depressed apex of a bridge, falling sideways, his arm punching through into space below him. The night carried into the next day, heat rising. Crevasses sloshed open beneath the skis as we slid over them. The final crawl into the airstrip was an escape from the jaws of death on the glacier.

All day the fog hung low, lunch bubbled on the stove, fresh bread was stacked into triple-decker peanut butter and jam sandwiches. 'I wouldn't count on your flight coming in tonight,' said Annie, who directed the planes. 'Clouds are just too low, they never get in when it's like this.' An hour later the hum of the Cessna echoed quietly up the valley, like a fly droning in a far-off cave. Then it appeared over the cloud in the valley. The plane nosed in around the corner, floated across the fog, then dropped, like a Spitfire going in for the attack, spinning down the face of the cloud and flaring out to touch the top of the runway, spinning and coming to a halt. 'Whew,' said Annie, 'I haven't seen that manoeuvre before.'

'Hi,' said the pilot, 'I'm Jay Hudson, thought you just might like a ride out tonight.' The cloud settled behind the plane, coffee was made, Jay returned with a beaver fur hat, a ruff of brown-flecked fur waving wildly around his face and in front of his forehead. 'Might have been a bit eager,' he commented. 'Might just sit here and see what those clouds do.' We swapped bush pilot stories and two hours later the cloud changed enough to be judged safe to fly, though only just. We clambered aboard with Kristof, a Polish climber on his way out. Sitting at the airstrip that afternoon, he'd mentioned casually, 'I was climbing last year, but got stuck up on the Football Field in a storm. The weather was terrible for several days so I hid in a crevasse before the Rangers finally got through in a break in the storm to rescue me. But I lost my feet.' I thought maybe feet translated to toes in Polish, but when he took his boots off later to show me, feet was an understatement. His prothesis extended far above his ankles to connect with his lower leg. A long recovery in Alaska followed by a return to Poland had made him determined to come back to McKinley, first to see the mountain and Alaska again, then for an ascent of the peak the next year.

Jay Hudson, junior, trained by his father and flying since the age of eight, flew with a light touch that piloted the plane like an arrow, nudging through the clouds, sensing the wind before it touched us. 'One Shot's closed now, we'll be taking Two Shot this time, but you might like it.' The plane curved up against the black rock, wings hovering off the edge of the cliff as if on wire. Two Shot was a loop around the low points of the ridge, curving sharply right, crossing a break in the cliff then back into a gorge. The cliffs rose up on both sides of the plane before it shot through into the valley and dropped away, down towards the forest below. It was more video game than flight. Dusk hovered grey under the clouds, rocks shadowed and dark crevasses cut the glacier below into cobwebs. The plane levelled out over the forest, floating in the gloom, the radio came on, the three lights of Talkeetna flashed by below and we landed like a leaf on the runway, the top of McKinley shadowed behind us.

Morning was contemplated from a motel bed, no snow to melt, no sled to pull, no McKinley to climb. 'C'mon Robert, I'll buy you one of those hats for climbing the mountain with me,' said Joe. 'Beaver ruffs, a man's best friend, we've got to have some.' Ruffs safely in their box, the train whisked us back to Anchorage, Bill Hammel was now in residence, returned from a fishing trip with his friend Tim Drisko. We swapped stories. 'Aren't you guys worried about bears?' I asked. Some innate part of me was curious about large carnivores and despite people always saying, 'Oh no, they are completely harmless,' the stories always seemed to surface which told a completely different tale. The newspaper I'd opened on the train told of an attack while we'd been on the mountain, in an article which wouldn't have won an award for subtlety.

WOMAN EATEN

The couple awoke to a scratching noise outside the cabin. The bear was becoming increasingly agitated, breaking the windows and beating at the door. The couple escaped out a rear door and onto the roof. While the woman distracted the bear, the man ran for the lake, jumped in a canoe and went for help. But by the time they returned, the bear had climbed a tree and caught the woman, killing her and eating her body before running off.

Tim had been sitting listening to the story quietly and left the room, returning shortly. 'This is what I use if those bears come after me,' he intoned. He brought his hand forward, revealing a pistol with a cannon-sized barrel, immense grip and dull glow of steel that held an aura of the old west when men were men and bears knew their place. Drifting down a river only accessible by float plane, fishing for the same thing the bears wanted to eat, made the pistol a very good idea. Having grown up on a farm in the American Great Plains, Tim had a natural enthusiasm for the outdoors that soon made us quick friends, as he later encouraged my training from his home in Vail, Colorado, calling with snow reports that any skier couldn't ignore, no matter where I was in the world at the time.

Bill Hammel had told me of another friend, 'who owns a bar, he's climbing the Seven Summits and you should meet him'. The 'bar' turned out to be Chilkoot Charlie's, an Alaskan institution built up over the years by Mike Gordon. With McKinley on his back doorstep, he'd made the climb several years before and then moved on to tackle the rest of the Seven Summits. Mike was a mixture of publican, philanthropist, mountaineer and art collector, the walls of his house lined with an art collection of astounding diversity, small prints set next to huge oils, one atop the other in a pattern that celebrated a wealth of artistic styles, every work adding to the next. His sense of humour extended to his wine cellar, where a model train wound amongst the racks to take the bottle of choice chugging back to the door. Alaska's backwoods image was dispelled with the first sip of Chateau Rothschild, bottled well before I was born, as we toasted the ascent of McKinley.

V

EUROPE

CHAPTER 18

AUCKLAND, LOS ANGELES, NEW YORK, LONDON, MOSCOW, MINRALNY VODY

JOHN STEINBECK IS FAMOUS for writing *The Grapes of Wrath* and *East of Eden*, but one of his best books is the little-known *A Russian Journal*. Preparing for his trip to Russia just after World War II with the well-known photographer Robert Capa he wrote:

> And it occurred to us that there were some things that nobody wrote about Russia, and they were the things that interested us most of all. What do the people wear there? What do they serve at dinner? Do they have parties? What food is there? How do they make love, and how do they die? What do they talk about? Do they dance, and sing, and play? Do the children go to school? It seemed to us that it might be a good thing to find out these things, to photograph them, and to write about them.

Fifty years later, the country may have changed, but what I wanted to learn was still the same. My curiosity extended to the people and their life, the countryside and the climbers we'd meet on our travels.

The details may have changed since Steinbeck's visit, but obtaining the visas and permits just to enter Russia was still a mountainous task in itself. Being in New Zealand, with arrangements co-ordinated through Mountain Travel in San Francisco, the Russian Embassy in New York and a Russian tour company in Moscow didn't help. Visas for Russia to climb Elbrus had to be organised several months in advance, with details of religious affiliation and a list of next-of-kin, and no explanation given as to what they actually needed this information for. Two days before departure for Russia, the visa came through, disappointingly sterile in my passport with nary a sign of a hammer and sickle in bold red ink. The South Pacific was left behind in a non-stop slide from New Zealand to Los Angeles.

The red-eye from L.A. to New York was a cultural event in itself, filled with trans-American commuters living between two coasts, not wanting to miss a day, cramming a five-hour flight, a three-hour time change and a full night's sleep into one plane journey. Tacked onto the end of an Auckland-L.A. flight, the red-eye was a hazy, sleepless event, surrounded by boisterous Americans talking self-confidently to new neighbours, stuffing suit bags into overheads with a vengeance, several arriving in something very close to pyjamas, their own large pillow in hand, dozing off with a Bloody Mary in one hand and a Jeffrey Archer novel in the other, a quick-acting sleeping pill taking them straight into dreamland. They missed the lights of Las Vegas, the Great Plains, the Mississippi and the Appalachians appearing as a black line across the earth before the lights of the east coast and dawn broke over the Atlantic. 'It is my dream to be reincarnated as a first class passenger with the seat next to me empty,' muttered the woman in front of me, who despite being in 1-A, had a junior movie star sitting next to her, his face buried in a madly beeping portable Star Wars game. She slunk back into the empty seat next to me and was asleep a moment later.

The night stretched into the ride north to Joe's house in New Canaan, taking advantage of the Connecticut limousine service to lie down at full length and sneak in an hour's sleep. The heat of late summer wafted in the car window and New York breezes compressed by the rush of wind filled the car, dragging dreams from New Zealand to New York. By 2 p.m., Joe and I were in suits and back in New York City for a meeting with Rolex, outlining plans for Russia and Antarctica. The heat of the day faded by the time we reached the Explorers' Club for a cooling beer with Phil Erard,

President of the New York Chapter of the American Alpine Club, and Terry Byrne, from NBC television, who had been supporting our video work on each of the summits. The Explorers' Club was a haven in the midst of New York, filled with an atmosphere of exploration past and adventures to come, a good place to share a drink and hatch plans. At sunset, Joe and I roared home to Connecticut, waking to a morning TV interview: 'Where is the top of Europe? In Russia! Is Russia Europe? What about Mt Blanc? How high is it? How do you get there? Are you scared?'

Not having looked at a map very closely, viewers could have been forgiven if they doubted we'd make it to Russia at all. All I did know was the climb was supposed to be easy and the mountain was located south of Moscow. With the newspapers reporting a coup a minute and the ruble losing value by the day, our pre-booked tour was designed to get us through the first week and then the trip would have to propel itself.

In New York's airport lounge I phoned London to warn Sandy Wylie we were landing on his doorstep for dinner. As the flight was called I placed a final call to Adventure Network, who would be flying us to Antarctica. 'Yes, we will save a space for you on the plane in December — but a cheque for airfare is due in 30 days.' Perhaps we could live on borscht in Russia and slide the budget along to Antarctica?

I'd first met Sandy Wylie in 1985 while working in Wellington. A Scottish stockbroker with a talent for investing large and spending small, in 1988 he'd kept track of the finances for my Everest Kangshung Face expedition, saving us US$5,000 in our first five minutes of conversation with the Chinese Mountaineering Association on our way through Beijing. This endeared me to his accounting philosophy: 'Of course it's possible! It just depends on the price, doesn't it?'

He'd since moved on to London, with a flat conveniently located in Holland Park. The only problem was his hospitality and social contacts guaranteed a perpetual stream of international friends in residence at any one time, putting even floor space at a premium. Luckily, Sandy's Scottish ancestry ensured a bottle or two of single malt was always in residence as well, allowing a nightcap or two to ease one into a deep sleep. Ed Webster was Sandy's only guest during this visit, another of my Everest teammates, just returned from a summer's climbing in Mongolia, with stories of snow leopards (and a film canister of fur he carried everywhere in his pocket to illustrate his story), snowy peaks and raven-haired Mongolian maidens, all an inspiration for our own travels east. Ed was going north to Norway in a few days and Sandy, having listened to Joe's and my adventures every time we passed through London, had agreed to join us in Russia, helping with the camera equipment and Joe's filming, while co-ordinating the travel details we planned to hatch once safe inside the borders.

Russia's official government tourist organisation, InTourist, would have liked to book us on a month's closely guarded tour. We'd settled for a week with a private company and stretched our visas to a month. We wanted to wander with no itinerary or set destinations, beyond a rough plan of where we wanted to go. Travelling freely around Russia was unheard of, but I felt Sandy's intrepid spirit and his British tenacity to explore the world would lead us through Russia to places a travel agent had never heard of before. Sandy Wylie had begun his travel adventures in his youth with a trip to America. Landing at JFK airport in New York wearing a kilt, he stepped outside the airport in one of America's less salubrious suburbs, put out his thumb and started a four-month hitch-hiking tour of America. This approach to travel seemed to be the ideal background for our tour of Russia.

At Heathrow airport the next morning, the distinctive tone of the Russian language and large men in dark suits who'd started the morning with a western cigarette and an East End mistress pervaded the boarding area. On the plane, the newspaper opened to a full-page story of Ed Webster's recent adventures in Mongolia, while a Bloody Mary calmed our nerves and we shot nervous glances at the other passengers. My incessant movement from continent to continent had made travel more and more routine, but with Moscow sliding in under the wings three hours later, dark buildings and motorways stretching into the distance of the forests, it felt a grand adventure, laced with fear, Russian passengers suddenly more prominent, English a forgotten tongue.

The airport was dark and had a dank smell, electricity on half power. Luggage flowed in on a clanking conveyor and a long queue snaked its way across the arrival hall towards customs. To the right a green arrow pointed through an uninhabited stall. I led the way through, later learning it was an exit no one ever took as everything needed to clear customs. On the far side, a slight young woman greeted us with a smile and a firm handshake, the first of a long string of beautiful and gracious Russian women we would have the fortune to meet. 'Hello, my name is Tatjana, you must be Robert, welcome to Russia.'

We had the bus to ourselves roaring down wide avenues, the grey cement block towers of a socialist success story and monetary failure lining the curbs. Belching Ladas and the infrequent black Mercedes cruised past. The hotel was a few blocks from Red Square, a reception area designed around the theme of a prison receiving room, clerks set behind glass. A narrow gold velvet couch lined the wall, heavy red velvet curtains and steel bars covered the dusty windows. After the gloomy entrance the rooms were surprisingly bright, in light colours, with a small fridge and white and modern bathrooms. French doors opened onto tiny balconies, towels were starched to stiff whiteness. We showered the flight from our bodies and retreated to the bar for our introduction to the Russian payment system.

The pub was supposed to be modelled after an English pub, but a hulking Vladimir behind the bar, the heavy gold velvet curtains and lack of beer on tap made the charade fade quickly. The only thing it did have was warm, almost hot, canned beer, paid for with three US dollars each. Our first week was inclusive of food, accommodation and travel to Mt Elbrus, complete with a tour guide. For this we handed over our US$1,600 each, in cash. At the end of the trip I counted up our funds again and realised that organised tours may have been comfortable, with everything arranged, but that the three weeks of independent travel following the organised tour cost us just US$400 each. But the tour would introduce us to Russia and ensure the opportunity to climb Elbrus before autumn weather turned to winter in the mountains. Tatjana casually tucked the $4,800 into her purse, a sum that would have kept most Russians in style for a few years, and led us off to Red Square.

'We were brought up to believe all Americans wanted to do was make war with us,' Tatjana commented as we wound our way through the streets of Moscow. Funny, that's the same thing the American government had told me, growing up in America. The American and Russian propaganda machines of the sixties must have all gone to the same school.

The buildings along the street had the grey weight that socialism seems to lend to construction. But sandwiched between the sombre towers were magnificent fluted and columned late 19th century examples, tributes to Czarist rule and grander times before the Russian revolution. On the streets, chugging Ladas and fuming diesel buses abounded, but by far the most interesting sight was the people. There was a distinct age difference, the older men represented by plain washed-out looking clothes, the victims of a cheap polyester factory. The younger men wore tailored suits and the briefcases were European, thin and black. The women would have fitted comfortably into any of the capitals of Europe, tall and stylish, with tailored suits and fine leather shoes.

Voices were confident, as if lifted off the L.A. to New York flight and dropped into Moscow. We turned the corner and stepped suddenly into Red Square. It was huge, the walls of the Kremlin lined the right side, Lenin's tomb tucked in underneath. St Basil's Cathedral, with its multicoloured spires, rose in an ordered heap into the sky. Russians and overseas tourists wandered the cobblestones, a queue led past Lenin's tomb, and an Asian group gathered in front of the cathedral for a photo as the light faded over the walls of the Kremlin.

Back at the hotel for dinner we found the dining room draped in more red velvet curtains, the ceiling ten metres above. A stage was set in the midst of the huge room and tables circled it in double tiers. Tatjana wound through the tables and groups of enthusiastic Russian diners. 'This is Sasha, he will be taking you to the mountain, and Nick Commande who will also be going with you.' Sasha would be our tour guide; his full name, Alexandre Morev, belied more of his heritage, his uncle in charge of dissidents at the KGB and his parents in equally commanding but never too-well-defined positions with the same organisation. Sasha had a strong face and angular bones, the classic Slav with rugged good looks, broad shoulders and a ready smile. His command of English and quick wit allowed him to derive humour from two languages simultaneously, ensuring a rapid and entertaining insight into both cultures.

Plates of sliced sausages, ham, beef, pork and cheese were strewn about the table, with eggs, cucumbers and tomatoes arriving as fast as they were consumed. Small glasses of sweet rosé wine dotted the table, fitted into niches between the plates. An hour later, a floorshow started, dancing girls in frilly feathered frocks twirling about on stage while huge speakers blared out timeless Hollywood tunes and the plates were cleared away. Just when dinner should have been finished, the main courses arrived, large steaming bowls of soup, followed by plates of meat and potatoes. Another hour of eating passed and desserts came swimming in, thick custards followed by coffee and more cheese. Sasha outlined our plans. 'We'll leave early for the airport, but the schedule isn't really set, so we'll have breakfast there and get on the plane whenever they call for us. It's about a two-hour flight. A bus will meet us and we'll have a short drive, lunch at a sanitarium, then onto the Baksan Valley at the base of Elbrus.'

It was still dark and the streets were quiet as the bus headed out of the city to the airport the next morning. At the back of the airport restaurant, a table had already been set. Omelettes cooling in grease arrived, the taste cut with liberal doses of pepper and endless cups of black coffee. An hour passed, and another, wandering from the restaurant to the waiting hall and back, passengers clad in dark colours trailing everywhere, seemingly caught in a travel void. Then Sasha called, 'That's us,' as the intercom blared and we shuttled suddenly through to a small hall and out onto the tarmac. The plane was immense and was boarded via a cavernous doorway set underneath and behind the wing. A tunnel led from the bottom of the plane, like a freight entrance, up into the passenger compartment. Alongside the stairs, racks held carry-on luggage in a self-loading system. The stairs zig-zagged up and back, climbing higher than a plane should be, opening out into a huge cabin, row upon row of seats stretching across the plane, more seats stacked up than in a 747. With every seat filled, the plane rumbled off into the sky. The Aeroflot trolls arrived with lukewarm tea and biscuits from a tray, nary a smile to be seen as they bustled up and down the aisles. Underneath, the plains of the Ukraine slid by, vast expanses of grassland turning to wooded hills as we dropped onto the runway at Minralny Vody, Mineral Water, gateway to the Caucasus mountains and Mt Elbrus.

CHAPTER 19

KGB BASE CAMP

THE BUS WAS WAITING, complete with Theo as driver, his assistant Boris, responsible for finding petrol and light bulbs, our own personal waitress Ludmilla, her assistant, and Sasha and his assistant Michael. This staff of six, which soon increased to seven, was all to look after Joe, Sandy and I, and the sole additional member of the tour, Nick Commande, a fireman from Racine, Wisconsin. Nick had become interested in the Seven Summits after an ascent of McKinley in North America, and had gone on from there to complete a peak or two a year, not only raising funds to climb them, but also for charity. He'd been to Elbrus the year before, but bad weather had forced a retreat, so he'd returned to have another attempt, with Sasha as his mountain guide.

With storms sweeping up from the Black Sea and across the Ukraine, bad weather was the most likely cause of failure on Elbrus. Mike Gordon in Alaska had told me about his two failed attempts in weather rivalling that which he'd experienced on McKinley, before he finally made the summit on his third attempt. Elbrus was close to 1,000 metres taller than any other mountain in the area, while also rising 3,000 metres above the plains to the north. High winds, cloud and drifting snow could quickly make an ascent impossible. During World War II, the Germans had occupied the same high camp we would be climbing from, and had set out symbolically to ascend to the top of Europe. But caught in a bad storm, they climbed the lower peak of the two headed summits, mistaking it for the top, and never actually reached the real summit at all.

The bus was a forty-passenger special with large comfy seats in Red Army velvet. It floated down the road with a roar, stopping with a whoosh of its air brakes. Dinner was on the outskirts of Pretigorsk, the bus winding up a thin lane lined with large trees and once orderly gardens growing rampant in the autumn heat. The sanitarium was a five-storey hotel with 100-metre hallways stretching in both directions from the small creaking lift. It was designed as a holiday retreat for one of the government departments, with an emphasis on recuperation and health. If the meal was anything to go by, sliced sausage, ham, chicken and pork followed by soup and a few tired vegetables dwarfed by a breaded steak flowing over the sides of the plate, rushing out for a game of tennis after the meal was pretty unlikely.

As darkness settled, the bus dropped further south, the plains flowing into hills and then rising up into mountains in the distance. We turned up the Baksan Valley, the village lights faded, traffic disappeared and pine tree air wafted in the windows. The bus crossed a bridge and then another as the valley narrowed. Headlights reflected off pines towering alongside the road. The centre-line faded into a thin strip of paved road snaking between the trees. Hidden hands pulled back an iron gate as the bus rolled up, a long deep squeak echoing from the hinges. 'Home,' said Sasha, sweeping his arm in the direction of what looked like an overgrown Swiss chalet. 'We'll get the bags, follow me and I'll show you to your rooms.'

Stone steps led to reception, which was empty, simply a large room with a tall ceiling and doors leading off it. A chandelier hung down through a central staircase, taken directly from a Munsters movie, complete with cobwebs. The floor was solid marble, the walls cement with a stucco finish in an off-colour pastel pink. Small lights in candle shapes hung from the walls, some flickering, some out completely. Sasha marched us up one flight of the stairs, then another, circling the black chain of the chandelier. A huge wooden door opened into an alcove and closets, then two doors side by side gave onto matching rooms. Each room had two tall single beds with a puffy-looking gold bedspread and thick pillows stacked up at the end. Doors opened onto balconies at the far end. To the side was the bathroom; no shower, but a large deep bathtub filled the back wall. Everything functioned just like every other hotel room in the world. Yet at the same time it was just a bit strange, creating an uncanny feeling of dislocation. Pastel colours were matched with the deep gold of the bedspread and curtains. The sink was pastel pink, the bathtub, which also seemed to be heavier and lower than it should be, a shade of forest green pastel, like a ceramic mix gone slightly wrong, and the floor was tiled in an off-brown. The medicine cabinet above the sink was square. Maybe Russia's equivalent of Philippe Starck had been responsible?

'Dinner in five minutes, downstairs in the dining room, I'll wait for you there,' said Sasha. 'Is there a key for the rooms?' I asked. Sasha looked at me and laughed. 'Robert, this is the home of the KGB, there are no keys and nothing to worry about.' After a few days we didn't even bother to close the doors.

Joe and Sandy and Nick and I met back in the alcove. 'This place is weird,' we agreed, as if a KGB decorator whose last job was a Siberian prison had been sent off with a large budget and questionable taste to design the KGB holiday dacha. The dining room could have held fifty people, but we were the only ones there, set around a long table underneath chandeliers, with china plates, crystal glasses and silverware lined up to the side of each plate. Another woman had joined us, tousled blonde hair and blue eyes set atop a large and powerful frame. 'This is Olga, she will be climbing with us and helping out on the mountain.' Olga smiled. We'd got used to people suddenly appearing, as if they were strangers, then when they had been around for awhile suddenly realising they were actually part of our group, as Olga had been, stepping onto the bus unannounced in the middle of the dark valley, like a mysterious passenger. It was a quality of Russia that things happened without our really knowing what was happening, never quite sure why or how the patterns fitted together. It seems that this had long been a quality of this country. I was reading a book on business in Russia that started with a quote from the Marquis de Custine:

> On entering the country of the Russians, one sees at a glance that the social order as arranged by them can serve only for their use. One must be Russian to live in Russia, although on the surface everything proceeds as elsewhere. The difference is in fundamentals.

The Marquis may not have been on an alpine holiday in a KGB dacha, but he had certainly understood what it was like.

The bed was long and the mattress sunk deep. The balcony door was propped open to let the breezes that snuck down the mountain by night into the room. At 8 a.m. breakfast was served: eggs, ham, cheese sauce and coffee in silver pots, Ludmilla our waitress already having learned our preferences for milk and sugar. 'All alpinists should have a personal waitress,' said Sasha. 'Think how little you have to worry then, your food is always arranged. The waitress runs the cook, the cook runs their assistant, but they are cooks, not there to look after you. So the most important person is your waitress.' It may not have been logic we'd heard before, but it was too comfortable to argue with.

The chairlift to the coffee shop had one-person seats that swung loosely beneath the cable, keeping our feet barely above the lush grass of the cow fields. As we ascended into the Caucasus on one side of the valley, Elbrus appeared up and across the valley on the opposite side, rising from 2,000 metres at the valley floor, into the glacial tongues curving down between the dark volcanic ridges at 3,000 metres, onto immense snowfields and crevasses at 4,000 metres, then up into the white ice reflecting the sun between the twin summits at 5,000 metres with a final thrust up to the real summit at 5,633 metres. It was immense, with the endless snow slopes and crevasses presenting a maze that in a storm would be deadly, the slopes exposed to the elements with little difference in terrain until the route was missed and a crevasse opened up underfoot.

From the top of the chairlift, a short walk led out of the treeline and up into the meadows, a lake shining deep blue in the sunshine. Peaks rose majestically behind, a setting worthy of the Alps, but without the trams flowing up their sides or the crowds at their base. Exercise was the walk back down, wandering from alpine tundra back into deep pine forests and out into hayfields set on terraces above the valley floor. A farmer waved his scythe, slicing through the grass in long gentle sweeps, a rhythm passed down from generation to generation. Lower down his wife gathered the grass and lay it over the stone fence nearby to dry in the sun.

Our petrol-finder and light bulb caretaker was Boris, a quiet man who shadowed Theo our driver. Finding petrol was a challenge in Russia, a constant battle between government coupons dictating quantity, a black market dictating price and the most basic problem, finding a station open with enough petrol to sell. Light bulbs were a mysterious commodity and we never learned if this was a serious consideration or one of Sasha's many inside jokes. But the box of bulbs tucked next to the engine on the bus was real, various sizes and wattages carefully wrapped in newspaper. At the dacha, lights seemed adequate, but later when we dropped into the heart of the Ukraine, Boris preceded us to our rooms to verify light quality. At the dacha he took on the additional task of adjusting the sauna, heating the rocks, checking the temperature and filling the water bucket. Returning from the day's hike, we'd wrap in thick yellow towels and descend through reception and down a shadowed hallway to the dark cedar-lined sauna. After we'd had a session of heat, the glacier-fed plunge pool outside turned us into ice cubes, followed by more heat until we retired to the tea room, with deep-seated couches and the samovar, to sip tea and tell stories, the atmosphere heavy with KGB history, imagining past guests murmuring quietly in Russian, hatching the latest world plot.

Sasha confirmed the dacha was used by the highest KGB officials, including Andropov during his reign at the top. It was strangely devoid of photographs or art, not a single piece gracing the wide walls. This added to the shell-like atmosphere, but in a world of spies, made it more difficult to hide bugs or cameras. Strangely out of place was a theatre with deep leather swivel seats and a five-by-eight-metre screen. Sasha had introduced us to the room with a hushed, 'This is the theatre where the agents would gather in the evening to watch Western films. Russian movies are terrible and they would watch all the popular Hollywood movies that nobody else could see, supposedly so they would know what decadence the West held.' Sasha's family connections to the KGB were obviously very strong, but when asked why he wasn't KGB himself he replied simply, 'I played and sang the wrong songs on my guitar.' That night he pulled the guitar from its case and we were treated to a concert of Russian songs, sung superbly, displaying a range and talent that had obviously been developed over many years, with a repertoire that moved confidently from the Beatles to popular Russian folk music, the stories translated with a laugh and an attempt at a rhyme into English.

With the weather still holding, the sky clear at dawn and red at night, we set out the next day for the tram to the hut where the ascent of Elbrus started from. In the winter, the slopes of Elbrus transform into a ski area, with trams taking skiers high up the mountain. By summer, the trams would whisk us up the lower slopes of the volcano, saving a long but easy hike up a winding dirt road that serviced the lift stations in summer. 'We will have an extra long climb,' Sasha said at the station, 'because the second tram crashed two weeks ago, landing all six passengers in hospital in critical condition, so the chairlift above is also closed. We will take the first tram, but then we will have to walk the rest of the way. But I may be able to commandeer a snowcat higher up.' Walking seemed like a good alternative to diving 100 metres inside a tram car into the rough volcanic rock of Elbrus.

The tram station was well-worn wood, the cable creaking suspiciously as it wrapped around the bull-wheel and stretched up the mountain. The tram held 20 of us comfortably, gliding out of the station and upwards, swinging and squeaking, bouncing over the tram poles 100 metres in the air, sliding into the next station with a thump. 'And from here, we are real mountain climbers,' said Sasha with an enthusiastic wave.

The trail wound easily up the mountain, gaining height rapidly, slinking between volcanic runnels and over ridges. The Baksan Valley opened out below, stretching along the Caucasus which ran down the far side, alpine peaks jutting abruptly heavenward, their tops nearly level with us across the valley. The coffee shop we'd visited the day before was a small dot on a meadow far away over the hills. At the snowfield the snowcat waited; packs, people and boxes of food were piled in and it ground up the slope to the hut.

Pruitt 11 looked like a strange airplane fuselage-shaped structure with a roof like a Conestoga wagon. The aluminium shell, shaped in a curve up the walls and over the roof, glowed dully in the afternoon sun. Another mysterious character, a short silent man in a thick woollen jumper who had sold us tram tickets, operated the buttons on the tram, then disappeared for a while before popping up again in the snowcat, now opened the door of the hut. 'This is the hut chief,' Sasha announced. The man said nothing, looking at us each in turn with no expression. The hut was known to be haunted; maybe he was the reason.

CHAPTER 20

BETWEEN BLACK AND CASPIAN SEAS

THE HUT'S EXTERNAL strangeness was only compounded on the inside. A small door made from a thick plank of wood kept out the mountain storms, backed by another door, which opened into a small alcove with shelves filled with hut slippers, exchanged for climbing boots on entering the hut. A feeble bare bulb flickered from beyond the room and a long stairway curved up and around to the first floor, past a long hallway and then on up to the top floor. Tucked in under the curving roof, the rooms were triangle-shaped, opening out from the doors like a thin slice of pie. A grainy porthole let in a ray of light at the end of the room over a small rickety desk suspended between two thin beds, one on each side. The walls were so thick that looking out the porthole was like the view from a submarine.

The dining hall was a floor below us, set on the end of the curving frame of the hut, just below our rooms. It felt like a crashed rocketship inside as well, which may have been the aerodynamic form the builders copied to make sure it didn't blow away. It was an immense structure to build so high on a peak, long before any helicopter could have dropped off the materials. It was of pre-World War II construction and looked like it had remained the same with few changes ever since. 'Those were the hot showers, just below the hut,' Sasha pointed out a frame of concrete and twisted steel below us. 'They were very impressive, the building they were in. So impressive that when they were bombed in the war, the bombers thought they must be the hut and so blew them up. So, so

139

sorry, no hot showers for you.' We'd just have to suffer. The volume of food we had grown accustomed to had followed us up the hill and a row of fresh-sliced cucumbers and tomatoes, roast beef, fatty sausages rolled tight in their skins layered on heavy white bread, followed by a stew, barnyard animals floating thick in the broth, warded off starvation. We waddled off to bed at 6.30 p.m. the weather crystal clear, a breeze whistling quietly over the rocket-ship.

At 12.30 I stepped outside, awake and ready to climb. Fears of bad weather were far worse than any desire to sleep. The sky was clear; stars were set against the white snow of the mountain like white Christmas lights. But it was still far too early to start the climb, getting lost on the slopes in the dark as much a hazard as getting lost in a storm. Back in bed, the thick blankets were still warm. I retreated into the cocoon and was up again at 3 a.m. 'I don't like the clouds in the east,' pointed out Sasha, creeping into the doorway behind me. A long line of black clouds against the horizon blacked out the stars over the Caucasus. With endless ascents of Elbrus to his credit and Master of Sport status, I didn't relish contradicting Sasha's advice. But knowing I could turn and run back down the peak if a storm approached, I didn't want to waste the good weather. 'I'll be going anyway,' I said. 'If the weather turns I'll be back down here right away.'

I'd already explained to Sasha my solo plans and that I was happy to climb on my own, even though on a peak like Elbrus, climbing solo is little more than semantics. As the mountain is relatively easy from all sides and usually climbed without ropes, the greatest comfort comes from being in a group or having a guide to keep you on track and out of the crevasses. Olga had already related the story of her boyfriend, caught on the mountain in a storm and disappearing down a crevasse to his death. Every time she mentioned crevasses her eyes grew larger and she shook her head. On the climb, Sasha would be guiding Nick Commande and Joe; I was on my own; and Olga would be looking after Sandy. But I knew that, realistically, if we all started at the same time, we could well be climbing fairly close together anyway.

'Well,' said Sasha, as we still stood in the freezing mountain air at the door of the hut, 'maybe we'll make a start as well then.' A coffee and a bread roll later Sandy and I were in the alcove, a room like a submarine's pressure hatch, where the boots went on before we rushed into the great outdoors. The hut was so comfortable that the first step outside was sure to be a shock. 'How do these crampons work anyway?' asked Sandy. I'd forgotten he'd never had crampons on before and the model he had, a reject from my previous Everest expedition, had been designed by someone who had obviously never had to put them on.

I strapped them onto Sandy's boots, which were borrowed from Joe and three sizes too big. 'How do I get the crampons off?' queried Sandy. 'Good question, I think you better just leave them on the whole way. They are too complicated to start messing with.' Sandy had a naturally high level of fitness, good sense of balance and was keen to climb Elbrus. But he professed to being frightened of heights. As a first climb, Elbrus perhaps wasn't ideal. I showed him how to hold his ice axe and he walked around the hut, crampons grating and catching in his pants, ice axe swinging, and quoting Sir Edmund Hillary from his first ascent of Everest. 'We'll knock the bastard off, we'll just knock the bastard off.' Then the snowcat driver offered to give us a head start on the day, so we all piled into the back for a ride out onto the snowfield. He soon came to a skidding halt, the slope and ice proving too much for the treads. We'd be expected to take at least part of the mountain seriously.

We were at 4,000 metres and had another 1,600 to go to the summit, still a respectable distance for a morning's climb. Olga seemed to have Sandy under control, or perhaps it was the other way around. Joe had taken a camera too many and fell rapidly into the rear guard with Sasha and Nick Commande. The darkness was illuminated by stars, the snow reflecting pinpricks of light, the air icy, cutting through my jacket. The slope was a consistent rise, crampons eating their way slowly up the slope. It felt like crawling, with no indication of upward movement.

A treadmill of snow extended into the darkness above. An hour later the horizon turned orange and then slowly tinged pink. With the sun rising, the shadow of Elbrus was cast onto the opposite horizon, the peak's reflection set darkly in the early morning atmosphere. The Elbrus shadow hung perfectly above the earth, a phenomenon I'd only seen once before, on Everest. Ten minutes later it was gone as the sun burned up out of the east and into the sky in a bound.

The route led left at the top of the slope, angling across to the col between the two peaks. I slid further left off the normal route and out onto the far ridge that led directly up to the rim of the volcano. Below, the snow led into the glaciers, down into a maze of crevasses, into the volcanic slopes and far off into the forests. From the depths of the Baksan Valley, the Caucasus mountains rose on the far side, alpine peak after alpine peak shooting up through glaciers and icefalls into pinpoint summits.

Volcanic ribs sprouted from the snow on the ridge, crampons grated on rock under ice. The sun rose in an orange flame, the wind jacket came off, then the fluffy jacket. I paused to film, setting the camera on edge, climbing up and down and up again over several sections, stomping through the snow with Russia spread out underfoot. The clouds that had heralded a storm over the Caucasus had melted, the sky was a clear slate of blue, bubbles of cumulus cloud floating lazily over the forest far below. The ridge ended abruptly in a final crest of snow, the rim of the volcano perfectly flat. Along the crater, Sandy and Olga toiled up the far ridge towards the summit, dots set against the white snow backdrop. The rim curved in a long gentle circle and the summit was a final bump on the ridge, a mound of snow higher than the rest. It was late morning, Europe spread out below, the Eiffel Tower seemingly just over the horizon. The sun was warm, the breeze light, the top of Europe as cultured and comfortable as the continent it stood on.

Sandy's big boots and crampons made him look like a duck as he came up to the summit. Leaning on the plinth that held the

bust of Lenin until a few years ago, he waved his ice axe enthusiastically. 'Of course, no one is more surprised than me to be here,' he
said expansively, then launched into a soliloquy that would have
made Hamlet proud as he pointed out the sights. 'The Caucasus
mountains form a natural barrier, which even in World War II the
Germans failed to breach, halting here in the Baksan Valley. Yet
even now, mortars are echoing over these hills as conflicts rage in
Georgia, just over there,' he said, waving his ice axe even more
expansively, 'and to the north lies the great breadbasket of Russia,
the Ukraine, which we shall shortly be crossing en route to the
Black Sea. Behind us, with just a little imagination, are the waters
of the Caspian Sea. And here we stand, suspended, between Black
and Caspian Seas.'

The altitude was obviously beginning to affect him. He pulled
from his suspiciously bulky pack the large pith helmet that I'd
picked up for him in Africa after climbing Kilimanjaro and posed
next to a deposed Lenin for a picture. I ate my own lunch, drank
my own water, the last vestiges of a soloist's integrity preserved,
and we trotted off down the mountain to the hut for afternoon tea,
passing everyone else toiling upwards in the heat, waving gaily,
laughing, 'The top's just over the hill, we'll go chill the vodka in a
few chunks of glacial ice,' sliding off down the slope with plumes
of snow shooting up in our tracks.

CHAPTER 21

FROM RUSSIA WITH LOVE

'RUSSIA IS FILLED WITH rocket scientists, we're all rocket scientists,' said Sasha. We'd been discussing why, with the high level of education in Russia, the light bulbs rarely worked and the soap wouldn't suds. Being a rocket scientist was Sasha's metaphor for explaining an over-educated intellectual population with no practical proficiencies. 'Dinner will be at eight tonight, so we'll start the sauna early — perhaps a bottle or two of champagne to replace your tea?' Sasha had been encouraging us to sample a little more of the local culture, starting with at least a small drink, which we'd been avoiding prior to reaching the top of Elbrus. Altitude and alcohol don't mix and going from 2,000 to over 5,000 metres in under 24 hours wouldn't have worked out quite so well with Russian toasts mixed into the bloodstream.

'What we need,' said Sandy, his successful ascent of Elbrus behind him and crampons off his feet for good, 'is the bus. I've spoken to Sasha. Without plans and an itinerary, we may have problems at the new border crossings, in towns and check stations. But if we have a bus, we at least look like a tour. We'll go back to Pretigorsk and Sasha will see if we can get the bus for a couple of weeks. Then we'll be our own tour. Who is going to argue with a 40-passenger bus?' The cork flew out of the champagne and we toasted our new tour. Sandy was right, who would question us? To round out the tour, Sasha suggested we take a few passengers, since we had the bus anyway. We'd grown accustomed to the comforts of a waitress and a driver who needed an assistant, and while

Sasha couldn't go with us, he had a friend who could act as guide, also named Sasha. The new guide became Sasha II, and he wanted to bring his wife and four-year-old son. Olga thought a trip to the Black Sea sounded like more fun than guiding on Elbrus, so she would ride along as well. The 40 seats were filling up fast.

Escaping the KGB dacha was proving difficult, however. Having climbed Elbrus well ahead of schedule we now had time for hikes from the Baksan Valley up into the Caucasus. We wandered up flower-strewn canyons between towering peaks to alpine pools for large lunches, a glass of vodka, a swim and a wander out to the sauna and dinner which stretched one day into the next. Evenings were spent playing billiards with the chief of the dacha, with toasts to Andropov and Nixon, the only foreign leader he knew. 'Perhaps we could get another look at the mountain,' Sasha proposed one evening. 'There is an Army rescue helicopter that might take us for a ride right around Elbrus, I'll see if they would like to do it tomorrow.'

At 9 a.m. the next morning a huge orange helicopter dropped into the valley and everyone from our group and a few extra locals materialised to scramble aboard. Inside there were rows of seats against the side and plenty of room for our ten-plus passengers. The pilot swept up and around Elbrus in a long slow circle, the mountain immense as we flew over it, glacier after glacier going by below. The porthole windows popped open so we could hang our heads and cameras out as the air rushed by and the glaciers whizzed past below. Then the helicopter curved off and down the spine of the Caucasus, threading through the spires, shooting over ridges and hovering past 2,000-metre ice-faces. We dropped back into the valley an hour and a half later, faces wind-burned from peering out the windows at 180 kilometres an hour.

The next day dawned with mist and rain creeping down the valley, the autumn storms arriving that I'd feared ever since leaving New Zealand. But with the mountain ascended, it was now safe to explore the lowlands. By noon the bus was loaded and we were on the road, winding back out onto the plains of southern

Russia. Mountain life faded, the big diesel pulled the bus over the rolling hills, the earth opened up as it escaped the confines of the valley, roads set between fields rolled for miles, the horizon blue and clean, set against sharply edged clouds that floated like balloons overhead. Barns the size of mountains grew out of the landscape. The feeling of moving through a huge field of food grew. The villages housed immense red tractors and large wooden farmhouses. Then the highway wound down, dropping as dusk settled towards the black of the Black Sea, dark water reflecting its name, but with beaches clean and white. Hotels had no signs, restaurants were non-existent. Ludmilla and Olga went shopping at the roadside market and came back with a leg of fresh meat, loaves of bread, jam, cheese and more sliced sausage. Soup soon bubbled away on the camp stove, fresh potatoes and onions were sliced thin and added to the broth. Apples, strawberries, watermelons and peaches were diced up and ladled with cream, big plastic bowls filled, crates came out of the hold of the bus and the table was set and tablecloth laid. Russian feasts were available at will as we curved along the coast of the Black Sea that night and into the next day.

At a seaside camp our southern exploration was halted. 'Mortar attacks to the south, not a great place for our tour, or my bus,' said Theo after talking to a passing truck driver, bullet holes still fresh in his windscreen. Ever protective of his trusty bus, polishing the windshield, blackening the tyres and polishing the chrome at every opportunity, Theo pointed the bus north. 'The Crimea, Yalta, the Lividia Palace, the holiday home of Russia,' said Sandy and a new course was set. Mortar attacks weren't part of our tour plans.

Sunset of the second day the bus cruised along a strip of elevated road set above a flat waterway, the peninsula extending out to sea and the ferry to the Crimea. 'Lie low,' said Sasha II, 'we are crossing into another place that thinks it is a new republic, they might want to see a visa.' Theo steered us into the special line for big trucks, transport vehicles and tour buses, the customs agent passing us with a wave and we were in, whatever this signified. Most of the new republics weren't quite sure what they were yet and the key was to keep one step ahead of their border regulations. Now we were somewhere, at least until we had to get somewhere else. Darkness on the Crimea settled, the road was a black strip with no lines or roadside reflectors, curving along high above the wash of the waves. The Russian Top 40 played in low tones on the stereo while sea breezes and the smell of cooling sand wafted through the windows.

'Very beautiful here, a beautiful night and tomorrow a more beautiful morning,' said Sasha's wife, a petite brunette with enough English to keep us marginally knowledgeable of our whereabouts as the bus tour slid rapidly off the map. Turrets like the great wall of China loomed in silhouette above the town of Sedak. A lone hotel with no sign and 500 rooms eventually admitted to having a spare one, stunned into disbelief at our arrival with no forward bookings. We snuck out from the hotel dinner and into town, a village by the sea with glowing coloured globes as streetlights and Moscovites on holiday wandering along the stone walk set above the beach. The restaurant was found by smell and noise, since signs were non-existent. Any place we'd found to eat was less than a year old, privately owned, existing in a grey area of the law outside the state food kitchens. Our one experience in a state restaurant had yielded up grey chicken flesh and green potatoes served by dirty trolls with dank hair and dirty, fatty hands with moss under their fingernails. They'd been banned from our tour itinerary, but finding the privately owned restaurants in a land where a simple sign is viewed as bourgeois capitalism required a lot of scouting ability.

A balcony over the beach yielded a rare find, a musician who owned the restaurant, eatable food, company to muddle through a conversation with. 'I want to get to know you,' sang the musician and later introduced himself the same way, curious as to our arrival. I couldn't place his speaking vocabulary until I realised, as he began an in-depth survey of Western music, that he had learned to speak English from the songs he sang. He entertained us into the late hours with stories told in 4/4 time, slipping into tunes from

Hollywood from the thirties and back to country and western as we talked of Colorado.

Our hotel was cleaning up from a banquet and floorshow when we returned, a lone table of workers finishing off a bottle of champagne and waving us over to join them. Joe retreated to the room but Sandy and I had no such reserve. Like entertainment industry workers the world over, their night life started when everyone else was finishing; a club was recommended, a Lada arrived at the front door and six of us were soon inside, a Russian Mario Andretti at the wheel, squealing back into town for a nightcap. With the town shutting down, we headed into the hills, curving far up into the cliffs above town, popping out on a ridge, the road diving back down towards the sea, threading cliffs on a skinny black road alongside compact rock walls. A Lada's suspension is suspect on flat ground; in S-turns it is like being in a rollercoaster, bottoming and then recoiling. The driver knew the road well or the car was lucky, shooting along the rock walls with sparks flying off the fenders being as close as he got to taking us to Lada Land, the place where all the crashed Ladas go. A village set at the base of the cliffs rose out of the dark. Tiny lights, a white strip of beach, a hard left along the shore, a few shadowy people suddenly appearing. The car shot right and screeched to a halt on the dock. Everyone out.

We were in an alcove from a fairy tale, rock cliffs rising a thousand metres behind us, with the beach, the village and a few hotel towers nestled above the sea. White waves lapped the sand, black water swelled back out into the sea. Old men sat on stools playing dominoes. A lone vendor at a stand, little more than a table with a few bottles set atop it, sold our driver a bottle of vodka, his supply running dangerously low with his new friends in tow. We wandered up the stone walkway set above the beach, minds intent on finding common ground while disparate languages kept creeping in and sending the conversation off on another tangent.

'This town is Novy Svet, the most beautiful village on the Black Sea,' said Alexandre, a tall blonde-haired woman with the best English of the bunch. 'Before the revolution it was famous for champagne and for holidays for the Czar's family. Its name then was Paradise, and some of us still call it that.' Even in the dark it looked idyllic, the remote seaside village approached by a cliff-side road framed by a moon-like beach of white sand and black sea.

The return to our rooms at the hotel was complicated by night maids roaming the halls, their security system a thin rope tied between chairs on the mezzanine, like something from a school camp; the Russian desire to keep tabs on people extended right into their holidays. Sandy and I made a dash past them and into the room, slamming the door. At times it was best to ignore the Russian rule-book. It seemed to be something the Russian people had been doing for years; we were just in the middle of a crash course. At dawn, coffee was in short supply at the hotel, an essential ingredient for starting the day. A quick walk down the hill and I spotted a coffee machine through the gates of a bar, striking up a conversation with the Armenian owner.

'The coffee will be on in a few minutes, it is good coffee from my home, there is no good coffee in Russia, please join me.'

The reassuring sound in the background was that of steam issuing from the Italian espresso machine, just like music. The Armenian was surprised to find us along the Black Sea. 'Russians, always Russians, and now they are always fighting. I come here, I start a bar like in every other country, they can't decide whether I should be open or closed, at what time, or what taxes I should pay. They know nothing of money, they are used to the government providing for them. But they don't want me to make any money either. But they will come to my bar because it is the best here.' The morning sun shone into the patio of the bar, a few more of our bar owner's friends arrived, a bottle of cognac was produced. 'The coffee is better for it, the taste you know?' We finally snuck away at noon, with a wave and an invite to return. 'No, no money, you have interesting things to say in a place that has little of interest, you are welcome any time.' His dislike of Russians and everything Russian had permeated every aspect of his conversation.

In the back of the bus, Sasha II had stowed away a few long

lengths of climbing rope which he now dragged out. The rope appeared to be rotting in the sun. He wandered off to the top of the nearby cliff over the sea and soon the ropes were dangling down the rock, kinked and with the occasional knot to tie off a particularly worn section of rope. Unlike modern climbing ropes, with a core and protective sheath, this rope had only a core, nearly worn through in places. I tied into a climbing harness wound round my waist made from what looked like seat-belt straps and started up the rock with a stronger than usual resolve not to fall off. Moving from the snow slopes of Elbrus to a vertical cliff that looked like a conglomerate of small rocks embedded in limestone was like changing from being a snowman to a gymnast. The tiny pebbles and crystals dotting the rock had to be caressed like cracked diamonds. The move from horizontal to vertical was instantaneous, the beach dropping away rapidly below, the Black Sea floating directly beneath me. Thirty metres up and the transition was complete, the mysteries of the rock overtaking the reality below, security dictated by pebble size and how much toe could be leveraged onto it. In the sun, the rock was warm and welcoming, the concentration required taking me from Russia to a simple reality, grasping tiny ledges, balancing from pebble to pebble, climbing up into an immense slab, beach set far below, cliff extending on all sides, a lone tree marking the cliff's summit far overhead. Sasha climbed with an exuberant style, sliding out to the left of the obvious line into a series of overhangs, the rock consistency deteriorating as the angle steepened. Suddenly a crystal popped loose underfoot and the rope stretched, wrapping tight around my shoulder as his full weight came on me. He bounced to a stop, the rope like a piano wire, pinging in the air. Sasha slid back onto the route and continued upward. I started breathing again, too accustomed to western rope techniques to trust the overgrown clothesline wrapped around my shoulders, Russian style.

As the sun set, we descended into the sea, the salt cleansing the cuts from worn hands and nicked fingers, floating in the dark depths. A black sea doesn't sound too appealing, but the black was more of a deep, dark midnight blue, curving around the rocks below the cliff, reflecting light-and-dark shimmers into the depths. Jumping in from the rocks, we found it cool and inviting, clear and deeply salty. The Black Sea had a reputation for being dirty, crowded and unappealing. Maybe InTourist just didn't take tours to the best beaches. The reality was white cliffs that could have come from Yosemite Valley, California, beach houses from the shores of Italy, the sandy beach from Florida and the sea from the Adriatic. What it lacked in tuxedo-clad waiters and cruising Corniches, it more than made up for in a feeling of remoteness, of being here before the dawning of international tourism and a wave of timeshare condos were stacked up on the beach.

With the risk increasing that our tour would stall on the beach next to a crate of vodka and a group of Russian friends, Sandy moved us on while quoting from an obscure guidebook. 'Yalta is the true gem of the Black Sea, set along the coast with a wide boardwalk along the sea, palaces from the days of the Czar and castles scattered along its length.' Theo changed from his bathing suit into his driving suit, the lounge chairs were stored in the hold of the bus and we wound back out from Sedak and west along the coast. The bus climbed far above the sea then dropped down again, the road widened, the sun grew hotter, the occasional palm tree sprouted from the roadside, hotels blossomed from the bay and, as darkness settled, we downshifted on the final hill into Yalta, a modern world of traffic lights, shops with signs and restaurants. The prominent tourist hotel recommended by InTourist was US$125 while around the corner a little persuasion convinced the local owner our tour was Russian, not international tourists, and we secured spacious rooms for us all with large terraces looking over the beach for a total of US$7.

The sounds of a late-night cabaret drew us off down a small avenue, a trio playing enthusiastically in a corner welcoming us. Dinner was several courses ordered by pointing at indecipherable lines on the Russian menu, resulting in yet another small banquet of meats in rich cream sauces and vegetables set in circular patterns on plate after plate. Unfortunately for the waiter, a surly chap who took offence at our being dragged off to dance with the local patrons and creatively added up our bill, Sandy could read numbers in any language. As the table still held the remains of our meal, he went over every plate, verified it with his newfound dance partner against the description on the menu and added up the total, a number reflecting a tenth of the waiter's quoted price. With pride destroyed and the patrons now howling in our defence, the waiter took a swing at Sandy, who, with his slight frame trained in Scottish pubs, ducked and crawled out rapidly between the tables, while his dance partner, a rather large and enthusiastic woman, bellowed at the waiter. I slunk after Sandy as the brawl erupted behind us, patrons checking their own bills and berating the management. Back at the hotel, Joe decided a night in was the best way to finish the evening but Sandy and I straightened our ties and went back out to continue the tour of Yalta.

The streets of Yalta are a European mix of French balconies, solid Germanic rooflines and the occasional cobbled street from Italy. The architecture drew us from one street to the next until we stumbled on the most incongruous symbol of socialism, a red neon sign poking out from the wall flashing 'Yalta Casino', an undertaking that any self-respecting capitalist tourist would feel compelled to support. We were welcomed through the large thick doors by two equally large dark men who showed us to reception. A tiny sign said '$5 chips, minimum entrance'. This was our daily travel budget, but after consultation with my accountant, we concurred this was an investment and couldn't be viewed as a true capital expense. This reasoning was faulty but, remarkably, turned out to be true. We stepped through another arched doorway into a room which seemed as if the proprietor had looked at every casino design book in the western world and incorporated the result into one small space. The ceiling was draped with light pink crepe, pegged up like an Arabian tent with thick gold tassels hanging down. The walls were hung with thick, deep red, velvet curtains, pleated in long folds and extending from ceiling to floor. The floor was white marble. The room was the size of a large private lounge which with the heavy decor created the feeling of a private boudoir inside an Arabian tent. A short bar was set into the wall at the back and an archway led through to a roulette wheel just visible to the left.

There were two blackjack tables and a craps table in the main room. As we entered, three tall women with black dresses cut low in front and flowing long at the back stepped forward to their tables. A barman came to attention behind the bar. A man in a tuxedo chatted with another equally elegantly clad in two low chairs in front of the bar. They regarded us with interest as we entered. That was it, though, there wasn't another customer in sight.

Soft music echoed from behind the bar. 'Let's play blackjack,' I suggested, the only game I felt remotely comfortable with. A tall woman with long dark hair and large brown eyes dealt the cards. Sandy and I nervously fingered our chips and watched the pile deplete slowly. Our five dollars had bought us stacks of chips, as they were in ruble denominations, so we were suddenly wealthy again, comfortable in our newfound affluence, probably about as stylish as an Arab with gold chains wearing a bedsheet and trailed by his harem is in Las Vegas. The dealer had a quaint habit of calling rubles *rubbles* and we soon realised she had only learned how to count to ten. As she liked to call out the number of 'rubbles' we had won or lost, we cut our bets to five rubles so she could continue to count the bets in English and the owner hovering in the background could congratulate himself on his staff training.

Playing blackjack with one other person and a dealer, no matter how beautiful, soon lost its appeal and we moved to the bar, sacrificing 200 rubles for a bottle of champagne. 'We need to try this,' Sandy said, stepping through to the roulette wheel. This was obviously more to the owner's liking and he stepped into position, the blonde taking up a position behind the table next to him while he manned the wheel. Sandy bet, the wheel spun, we lost. He bet, we lost, he bet, we lost. Then he pondered and I could see his accountant's calculator whirring. We were down to our last ten rubles. He bet. We won, and again. Then the chips were stacking up, against long odds, and the pile grew back to twice its original size. 'That's it, back to the bar.' He whispered to me, 'All we want to do is cover drinks, I don't think we want to push it.'

The owner joined us for a drink. 'One month, my casino, new in Yalta, do you like?' We nodded enthusiastically. Sandy began talking numbers. I turned to see a large man of about fifty with light hair step through the door, closely followed by a woman with red hair who was 15 years younger. He approached as if we'd already met, ordered champagne, greeted us cordially and then leaned back on his heels and as if from a stage delivered, 'Ah, an American, a Scotsman, right here in Yalta. We should drink to that!' With a flourish he pulled the standard pint of vodka from his pocket, where all Russian men seemed to keep a reserve supply, waved at the bartender for glasses which were duly produced as if on cue, and, 'I was a MIG pilot,' he said, 'but now I live quietly with my wife and family. This is my mistress,' he nodded and smiled at the woman next to him, who introduced herself. We toasted each of these events. More stories were told and Sandy invested more earnings in champagne. I snuck back to the blackjack table to spend some more rubles and evade another round of toasts with the MIG pilot whose stories were circling the globe with a geographic and political knowledge that seemed far too accurate to be all make-believe. The blackjack game, me versus the brown-eyed beauty, was going along so well that soon I couldn't help but increase my stakes to five chips of 10 rubles each, then five chips of 100 rubles each. Chips mounted, fell and climbed again. I cashed some in and went back for another round. The owner was laughing and drinking at the bar with Sandy, the MIG pilot and the mistress. I filled my pockets one last time from the cashier, tipped the dealer enthusiastically and with only a few shreds of darkness left in the night, Sandy and I crept back to the hotel.

The room felt claustrophobic and, remembering the balcony, I pulled the mattress off the bed and retreated outside to the terrace where sea air and gentle waves lapped below on the shore of the

Black Sea. I awoke to bright sun and Sandy sitting on the floor next to me counting stacks of rubles. 'That was a great night and we have come out rather well. You've just paid for another week on the road. As your accountant, I'll take charge of this. Now get dressed, we are off to the Lividia Palace, site of the most important meeting after the war.' I didn't feel like pointing out to Sandy that I was already dressed, an oversight from the night before.

Perched on a promontory overlooking the Black Sea on the outskirts of Yalta is the Lividia Palace, once a holiday home for the Romanovs. It was overrun by peasants in the Russian Revolution and was then the meeting place for Stalin, Roosevelt and Churchill at their historic carving-up of Europe. Shoes were traded for low-cut rope slippers at the door, the wooden floors led through archways and down hallways to empty rooms with tall ceilings and long thin windows looking out on the sea. Devoid of furniture, it was also devoid of atmosphere, only a grainy photograph of the table in the meeting room providing a hint to its historical significance. But around the back was the Romanovs' private church, filled with relics, atmosphere and that musty church smell that almost recreated the Czar's family kneeling at the altar in the dim light that filtered through the grated windows. The feeling of a culture at its height 70 years ago, suddenly put on hold, business, dreams and enthusiasm brought to a shuddering halt, wrapped up in cobwebs and left to rot, permeated the Palace, like so much of Russia.

Tourists in Yalta, a day later we yearned for the wild west excitement of the Russia only Russians knew. We'd grown used to battling for hotel rooms, picnicking alongside the road and befriending incredulous Russians filled with enthusiasm at finding their first Westerner in out-of-the-way places. Our stop at the beach had been far too fleeting and the tiny village at the end of the road over the cliff was calling us back. Theo was more than happy to oblige and our group of passengers was happy for a return. So we left Yalta, curving back up and along the sea and over the hill again. The narrow twisting road was a challenge even for Theo, but he squeaked the bus through the rock walls and into Paradise as darkness settled. After a hunt through the village, we discovered a beach house, two-roomed, built in the shape of an octagon. The rooms were panelled with light timber, walls inset with dark strips of lacquered black and red wood. The ceiling swept up to a point in the centre, like something from a gothic tale, and all for US$4. We were back at home on the beach.

In the hunt for breakfast the next morning, we struck up a conversation with two tall and lithe Russian women, Katr and Irena, whose rudimentary English belied an intelligence far beyond their language capabilities. Perhaps they were rocket scientists? The conversation extended over coffee, where we bumped into the first person we'd met who was fluent in English, Ramill. His opening words were, 'Where did you come from? I can't believe you are here, how did you get here? I've been coming here for 17 years and never once met anyone from the West.' Ramill was from Moscow, a businessman in 'import-export', and was quick to relate tales of his travels abroad. His short compact frame, dark tousled hair and beard set below beady brown eyes made him look naturally mischievous. But as the only English-speaking person who knew the area, he was to prove an ongoing source of information. Pleased with the chance to speak English, Ramill was happy to translate when we struck up a conversation that stretched beyond our limited capabilities.

'Do you always eat french fries for breakfast?' queried Katr. When on our own, our eating habits had adapted to bread and potatoes, always a safe choice. It was nearly noon anyway, so following up the french fries with toast would have balanced the meal. Katr waved her hand and called the waiter, spoke at length to him, consulted the menu, queried again, waved at us, and the waiter bustled off to the kitchen, returning minutes later with the first course of the tableload of food that was to follow. 'You do not understand Russia too well,' said Katr, looking at us like we were small boys. Her friend Irena nodded and they chatted amicably while we ate our first decent breakfast in a week. 'In Russia,' said Katr, 'you must demand what you want, you must tell people to go get it at places like this, otherwise you get nothing.' Rain started outside, dotting the stone beach walk with a fine mist, the restaurant filling and emptying as early bathers retreated to the large hotel dining room for their set lunch and an afternoon nap. 'What shall we do tonight, then?' asked Katr, and our Russian tour passed into more capable hands than our own.

Back at the bus, a rendezvous with our Beatles-speaking, restaurant-owning friend was planned. We'd discovered a Russian champagne, 1984 vintage, that we had developed a fondness for. Russian champagne had been developed from the French a century before and maintained many of it qualities, this variety very close to a vintage Taitinger with an extra rosé tint of colour. Our travels had yielded the occasional bottle, but what was required was a bulk purchase. Pulling into Paradise we'd come upon a mosaic set next to the town square, depicting a woman surrounded by champagne bottles. Set above town below the cliffs, a long low house sheltered in the midst of a field of grape vines. A return to the restaurant confirmed the champagne of choice and the vintages from Paradise were one and the same. 'It will be expensive,' said the restaurateur, shaking his head sadly, 'especially the vintage, it is quite rare, but I may be able to get you some.' A day later three cases arrived, for which we parted with just over a dollar a bottle. Because restaurants often proved both elusive and difficult to order from, we supplemented our potatoes and bread with cans of beluga caviar. Adding champagne to the menu would round out our diet.

Dinner was at a beachside café where, assisted by Katr and Irena, we enjoyed a real meal, barbecued chicken, fresh salads laden with cucumbers and tomatoes, potatoes and the first of our champagne, the tiny bubbles slipping down like fresh spring water. Katr and Irena were in evening dress, befitting the elegance of their Moscow heritage, barely recognisable from the morning's beach attire. The moon slid up out of the Black Sea, golden above the dark water, waves lapping below the restaurant. The rain had cleared and white clouds scudded along the horizon, forming dark pools of light over the sea. A wander down the walkway took us back along the beach, people moving back and forth in a steady stream, promenading in the cool evening air. 'In the evenings Russians like to walk and talk together,' said Katr. 'We discuss life and loves.' The open-air gazebo housed the disco, a low-key event of beachgoers wandering off the sands, through the atrium and up the steps to lean against the rail set above the sea, watching the moon sail higher while the music washed out of towering speakers and into the cool night air.

The sea was flat for an early morning swim, paddling out deep into the bay, the biggest ripples floating off the few swimmers up for a pre-breakfast dip, circling the fishing boats anchored far out in the bay. By noon beach life had slowed and the cliffs hanging above the village beckoned. Skipping the Russian climbing rope, I slid back to the bus for rock shoes and chalk bag, wandering up the road to the largest cliff. The earlier climbing with Sasha II had tuned hands and feet to the rock and balance returned immediately, moving the mind from horizontal to vertical. The cliff was 300 metres high and twice as wide, the rock sandy but solid, pale yellow with streaks of water-washed slabs set in black. At the edge of the black strips the rock had been cleaned by centuries of water, but still held pockets and tiny fractured ledges. A steep corner led up into the middle of the face, where a terrace and a tree provided a place to sit and look down at Paradise, Black Sea curved against the white beach, set like a crescent moon against the water. The village crawled up the hill behind and into the cliffs above, before the light blue of the sky curved overhead. From the terrace, the cliff steepened. What had looked like a wide face narrowed into a rib and then forced a traverse into another steep corner. The footholds disappeared as shoe soles slid out flat against the opposing walls. Edging up, not wanting to retreat, first thinking of having to start again, then disliking the added danger of climbing down. The holds returned, the left wall revealed a thin crack, a fingerhold; I moved quicker, knowing there would be no retreat now; the crack widened, a hand, then a foot, jammed tight. Finally a ledge big enough to rest half a shoe felt like a sidewalk had suddenly appeared. Then another traverse, a small brown lizard following me across, a curious neighbour savouring the heights. A final long corner swept up and around, the angle slid back, the summit ridge appeared, a final step, the top. An hour later I was back on my towel on the beach, hardly missed. The smell of hot rock was on my hands, toes cramped and sore from the tight rock shoes, chalk dust in my nostrils. 'This climbing is like Russian ballet,' said Katr, 'the movement, and you must have strong toes, yes?' Barefoot on the beach, at least the toes I had left weren't doing too badly.

Late afternoon we rejoined the tour bus, freshly polished and windows shining, crawling up and over the cliff and out of town. We waved out the back window, 'See you in Moscow,' to Irena and Katr. Three hours later we stepped off the bus, farewelled our crew with hugs and tips and leapt onto the train as it left Simferopol for Moscow. The first class cabin was grey, bunks hard, two to a side. Our cabin mate, in describing what he did, kept putting his fingers, crossed, in front of his eyes and peering through them as we endeavoured to learn his profession. Sandy at last got it. 'We are riding through Russia with a guy who's just got out of prison.' It was a blessing in disguise, as we enjoyed the man's company and stories and the seedy train conductor left us alone when the ex-prisoner growled at him as he started to bother us.

The next morning, our convict left and the train conductor came back, stoked on vodka, demanding a bottle of our champagne. Joe slammed the door and locked it, only to be faced with the return of the conductor with a train officer. He entered with a pass key and we soon understood that he was even more intent than the conductor on collecting gifts. Diplomacy failed. Volume went up. The conductor was manoeuvred outside. The officer sat down for a quiet chat with Joe, placing his hand in a brotherly fashion on Joe's leg. Joe, mild-mannered and gentlemanly at the worst of times, growled, and reverting to Navy training, grabbed the train officer and threw him out, slamming the heavy steel door. There was a howl from the train officer, his hand cut and bleeding, smashed by the door, then the door rebounded and he fell back into the corridor outside. Joe slammed and locked the door. Silence. The next three hours were spent wondering if a larger force would return and we'd be carted off to the gulag. But the train eventually chugged into Moscow, the grey and brown and black of the city increasing as we slid through the outskirts and into the station.

Maybe it was the return from the idyllic beach life, but the Russian train station was like entering an unwashed mausoleum. Low-flickering bare bulbs lit the tunnels under the tracks that led into the station. Dark and dank passages, with people lying in puddles in stinking clothing, lined the stairs which led up into a great hall, the ceiling a huge arc overhead. From it hung great lights on heavy black chains. The structure was incredibly elegant, with fluted columns, blocks of rock carved into towers, and the ceiling curving far up into the heights. But from the stinking floor up, it was an elegance wiped out by layers of dirt smudged onto the walls as high as people could reach, then dust and cobwebs festooning the columns. The lighting cast a dull grey aura over everything, dark shadows hovering in the corners. Worst of all were the people, vacant-faced bums wandering without reason amongst travellers with suitcases dragging along behind them. It smelled like a cross between a dirty toilet and an old unwashed locker room. Our original guide, Sasha, had been phoned to meet us, but was nowhere in sight, nor did we know where we were supposed to be staying.

Cast adrift in Moscow and still recovering from the train journey, I finally wandered out on the street in front of the station. 'Robert, so there you are, welcome back to Moscow, how was your trip?' Sasha greeted me, rescuing us from a night wandering through the streets. Moscow at midnight with no place to stay would have been an adventure not worth having. The train ride had taken 26 hours and cost a dollar, first class. The return to the tourist hotel was true luxury, a room booked and a private bath, safe from vodka-wielding train conductors.

The following evening we were suited up and in front of the Bolshoi Theatre five minutes before the performance started, Sandy negotiating for black market tickets. 'The longer we wait, the better it is. Don't be fooled,' he said, as scalpers discreetly touted for our business. 'They have obviously got the tickets, the closer to curtain time we get the less they are going to cost. We are trading in a falling market and as soon as the door shuts they'll be left holding worthless paper.' The theory worked; we traded a quarter the money for tickets we'd been quoted on our arrival and as curtain call echoed through the doors, made a dash inside.

The Bolshoi Theatre is in the heart of Moscow, an ageing building in Greek style with white columns rising to a peaked roof with galloping horses cast atop the crest. Inside, stairs covered with faded red carpet led up and around through narrow hallways, then burst suddenly out into the theatre itself. The main auditorium extended below, then the stalls were racked up in tier after tier, boxes extending out from beside the stage. The lights dimmed. An hour later they went up and steps led to the bar for a glass of champagne. 'You like it, yes?' asked Katr. It was the kind of performance that makes one slightly numb, left to marvel at human imagination and the beauty of the body in motion.

Another hour passed just as quickly, then another. The Bolshoi still deserved every bit of its reputation, ancient curtains and flaking paint aside, the performance was pure art perfectly performed. We retreated across the street to the Metropole Hotel, a long-established institution with flowing wooden railings, stained glass and a dining hall graced with art and statues, for the post-theatre dinner. That the train station from hell and the ballet from heaven existed in the same city stretched the imagination.

The train clanked north the next day, the official Moscow-St Petersburg tourist train with private cabins, nets for clothes, sinks that popped from below tables, shelves that slid out over the bed, tiny reading lights, double-thick pillows and down duvets eclipsing the historical nightmare of the previous train journey. Was there a constant in Russia? The taxi drove miles through the streets of St Petersburg to a hotel on the outskirts of town. 'No,' we said in a loud voice to the tour agent, who replied, 'But it is impossible, you are lucky to have a room,' at which, veterans of the road, we got out the book, phoned around and located a hotel in the city centre, on the river, with rooms with a view, and were back in the taxi, escaping from the grey Russian suburbia.

Along the river, wide stone walkways were set with thick stone walls dropping into the river. Broad avenues reached across to dark stone buildings, the rich reds and yellows of hewn stone rising up into arched windows with metal-grated terraces. Street after street was filled with pre-Revolution buildings capturing the best of European architecture. Like everything in Russia, these were massive structures, taking up city blocks, with archways leading to court-yards filled with Orthodox churches. Wandering the streets was an endless odyssey of discovery, like sailing through a Grand Canyon of culture. Few people were about, few cars were on the roads, the clip-clop of horses' hooves and a carriage from *War and Peace* seemed just around the corner. Stairs led high into church towers and winding ramps led down to terraces set above the broad canals. Gold domes glowed at sunset.

Dinner was with two Russian students, friends of friends from Paris, enraptured with the West, curious. 'I would just like to work in a professional office, where everyone wore suits,' Natasha intoned, recently returned from Paris, unhappy with her colleagues' dress sense. Her friend was quieter but smarter, with large brown eyes and flowing dark hair. What had been told about Russian women must have been seamen's stories from Vladivostock and Murmansk, as we were yet to run across more than your average amount of the larger type with hairy forearms and moustaches we'd been warned of. Instead, we kept meeting women who were quietly sophisticated, of high intelligence and, lest we overlook the obvious, great beauty. With more than 20 million Russians killed in the war, primarily men, day-to-day life in Russia seemed to be run by strong and intelligent women. Men were more frequently seen in consultation with their friends and the ubiquitous vodka bottle.

The following day we wandered in the back door of the Winter Palace and through rooms of Monets, Pissaros, Renoirs and Van Goghs so numerous that some hung sideways in corners, as if they were about to be carted out to the back room. Lights, as ever, flickered, a row of windows cast long shadows over the creaking floor and cobwebs hung in profusion from the ceiling. The sale of any one of the paintings would have built an entire art museum anywhere else. A few people wandered past, but the museum was nearly empty, with space to wander right up to any painting and stand silently as long as we wanted. Leaving St Petersburg we left behind the gem of Russia, only the surface of a city diamond scratched.

For the first time on the trip, Joe, Sandy and I split up, Sandy off by train to Finland, Joe staying in St Petersburg to photograph while I returned to Moscow. I went for a final dinner with Irena and Katr, finding one of the new and secluded private restaurants tucked away behind the offices of the official Russian news agency TASS, where Katr worked. Seven small tables, archways and draped curtains over the front window created an intimate atmosphere, the waitress a daughter of the proprietor, her mother the cook. A salad with a light dressing, ringed with tomatoes and cucumbers, plates of sliced meats and cheeses, thick creamy soup with slivers of meat and chicken surrounded by fresh vegetables, each arranged on a plate of their own flowed out of the kitchen over the next two hours. Irena, on an enforced English course since she met us and a computer programmer by profession, had learned more than I had with my phrase book in hand for the last month, so conversation flowed in circles for the first time, aided by a last bottle of vintage champagne. Over coffee Katr charted my future based on numerology, matching birth date and time to my character and upcoming events. She only told me half of it, I'm sure, reserving the rest to contemplate on her own, leaving me knowing far more than before, but still with a mystery, the full picture shimmering unseen beyond the edges, like Russia itself.

CHAPTER 22

STREAKING THROUGH DEEP PURPLE

Moscow receded on a rainy autumn day, the country fading like a dream, the beginning and end of the story marked by the flight in and the flight out. We'd met the people, we'd talked of life and love and war. We'd discovered more similarities than differences and we'd made friends we'd remember for a long time. London was warm and welcoming and we suddenly realised that Russia, no matter how friendly, had always been a bit uncertain, as if something we had no control over might happen and we would wake up in Siberia instead of on the beach. Flights to New York were full but I went to the airport anyway, wanting to be back in America, with all its familiar solidity. I stood by for three flights but luck wasn't with me. I resigned myself to another night in London. The British Airways ticket agent was in the process of booking me into a hotel for a lonely night, when someone with more stripes on their shoulder arrived behind the counter and peered over her glasses at me.

'Why did you miss your earlier flight?' she queried in that British accent which made it sound like I had missed an appointment with the Queen. 'In 1988 I led an Everest expedition with one of your compatriots, Stephen Venables, who became the first British person to summit Everest without oxygen. He's just returned from India with two broken legs and I had only one chance to see him. I decided to stay an extra night and take my chances today.'

'And where are you going now?' she asked. 'New York,' I said. She leaned forward over the ticket agent and said, 'How's that flight look?' 'One seat,' he replied.

She peered over her glasses at me for one last look. 'I guess you like adventure. We've one more flight today and it leaves in ten minutes. You'll have to run,' and she handed me my boarding pass.

I ran. Overweight briefcase and camera cases cleared a swath as I swept through the hallways of Heathrow, into one end of the lounge and out the other.

'Mr Anderson, so pleased to welcome you on board, just watch your head.' I stooped through the small door and turned to make my way down the aisle.

My first thought was, 'This plane is too small, I'll never make it to New York on this.' Then I second-guessed even being on the flight. Maybe it was the flight back to Moscow? I got a good look down the endlessly long aisle, the grey leather seats, the stainless steel gleaming amongst the dark colours, the whispered tones of passengers clad only in natural fabrics and gold watches and suddenly realised I could only be on the Concorde. I'd entered the hallowed club that flew 20,000 feet higher and over twice as fast as everything else. I walked the length of the centre aisle to the last row and the last seat.

The seats, two abreast on each side, were little larger than a standard seat, but with double the leg room. And something about all that grey leather and stainless steel, with the attendants in tuxes carrying silver trays, made the atmosphere much more akin to a corporate jet than a commercial airliner. The seat was next to a small window, more of a porthole really, with three layers of glass. The plane was full, 100 people ensconced in a long thin aluminium tube 203 feet long, as compared to a 747's 231 feet. We were pushed away from the gate and the jets fired up, a rumble completely different from a normal jet. The wings were huge, flat, big enough to build a house on. The flaps stretched like vast butterflies off the tail end, flexing their muscles as we purred out to the runway. The pilot came on, speaking in hushed, reserved tones, providing novice supersonic fans with the details while quietly paying homage to that élite group of Concorde frequent flyers who travel London-New York and back for the day.

'The Concorde weighs 181 tons and we'll be taking off with full thrust using our afterburners. This will take us from standing to 100 miles per hour in 1.9 seconds. After 82 seconds we'll power back to reduce noise and cruise up to 28,000 feet. I'll update you just before we go supersonic.'

The Concorde rolled to the end of the runway, 181 tons of perfectly stressed metal, riding like a brick-solid sports car. It sounded like we were already flying, the sound of the engines a loud roar, coursing up and down the scale as they warmed for take-off. We turned the final corner and lined up as the cabin grew quiet with anticipation, even the regulars tense. Unlike a big jet, which seems to set off down the runway with a lot of noise, loping slowly up to speed, the Concorde went straight from a solid roar of power to the physical realisation you are flat against the back of your seat. The rush of exhilaration was like the first big hill on a rollercoaster that you go screaming down, arms in the air, as a child. The man next to me, a greying, long-haired entrepreneur who'd 'popped over for the day for a business lunch' unsheathed his Compaq computer and just before he fell to work said, 'I reckon you get your money's worth just on the take-offs.'

That was the only thing he said for the remainder of the three-hour flight. We settled back for a quiet ride out over the Irish coast, staying just below Mach 1 (660 miles per hour) to avoid sonic-booming the countryside into oblivion. In the back of the seat was a soft, dark grey leather folio, containing embossed Concorde stationery, silver pen and leather notepad. The flight attendant arrived, dark, petite, slightly mysterious, very elegant. The champagne was 1981 vintage, the crystal twinkling in the tiny cabin lights. Everything in the Concorde was carefully sculpted, compact, from the cabin lights to the contoured seat-belts. At the front of the cabin a subdued digital readout glowed lightly green, indicating speed and altitude. A few minutes after take-off the Captain came on again.

'We'll be going to Mach 1 at 28,000 feet. However, you won't feel a thing. We'll then continue up to our cruising elevation of

57,000 feet at Mach 2 and proceed across the Atlantic to New York. Flying time will be just under three and a half hours.'

As the lights of Ireland faded below, any fishing boat below heard the first sonic boom as the plane passed the speed of sound, then a second boom reflected off the lower part of the nose cone. The nose tipped up and headed for the stars. Champagne and caviar arrived, taking me back to Russia. I wandered forward to see the rest of the plane, all one aisle of it. The door to the pilots' cabin was open and I edged forward. A uniform-clad officer motioned me in and said, 'I can't talk as we are a bit busy now, but just have a look if you wish.'

The cockpit was swept back like a jet fighter, the nose extending miles in front, an arrow pointing at the black sky. The world curved off into an endless horizon as we headed towards the outer atmosphere. The stars were bright white and had lost their earthly flicker. Behind them, the sky had gone to midnight black, an intensity of space hovering at the tip of the nose cone. Back inside the cockpit the walls and ceiling were lined with instruments, tiny switches and digital readouts in precise rows, glowing quietly in the darkness.

I retreated to the comfort of my main course, roast duck in orange sauce, a wine bottled before I was born.

Passengers were a mix of British and American with a few other nationalities thrown in. They were predominantly businessmen and a few couples, the power of money and time self-evident.

Out the porthole, the sun was coming up for the second time that day, but in the west. Flying twice the speed of sound, we were catching the sun. It rose purple orange, like a morning on Everest. The clouds caught the western sunrise, laid out like flat fluffy waves, rolling across the earth. Above, space spread to dark purple streaked with orange and the sun, a floating ball of flame, emerged through the black haze of New York. The silver of the harbour and the sea reflected heavenward, like glistening branches laid on a black earth. Jet engines powered off to resting pace as we returned to earth. The wings held up the thin plane body, settling us gently towards landing like a flying carpet. New York floated on the edge of the Atlantic, the crisp outline of the skyline hovering over Manhattan Island. The Concorde spiralled down in one long high-speed loop, my only regret the flight was too short and Russia was now so far away.

VI
ANTARCTICA

CHAPTER 23

SOUTH TO SOUTH AMERICA

A VERTICAL KILOMETRE above the glacier the climbing became more difficult. The hard snow turned to ice. The black rock squeezed the climb into a skinny icicle of existence. Only the front points extending straight forward from the steel-toed crampons separated me from a very long slide onto the glacier. The ice was blue and crisp, ice tools penetrating a centimetre. A very gentle flip, almost like the cast of a fly-fishing rod, set them into the ice. Then the toes followed, like ballet, a few centimetres higher each time. The air temperature was steady at 40 below zero. At 4,500 metres elevation, every intake of breath froze into the back of the throat and dripped icicles into the lungs. Yet, at 2 a.m., the sun was high in the sky, blazing almost. But heat was non-existent, the sun a ball of flame casting an orange light thousands of kilometres over the ice, illuminating crevasses, throwing shadows through the sastrugi and highlighting the nunatuks. The world of ice was remote from earthly reality, even having its own vocabulary.

The temperature on Mt Vinson started at minus 20 and went down. High on the peak the winds started at 80 kilometres an hour and went up. Exposed skin turned white in seconds and black blisters formed the next day. The closest full-time civilisation, if it could be called that, was the South Pole, nearly 1,000 kilometres further south.

Two weeks earlier, in the midst of packing for Antarctica, it was those fears of the ice and cold and wind that had me on the phone to Jay Smith saying, 'I've never done so much planning and packing, it's even worse than Everest. I'm just not sure I've got the right gear, or the right food. Do you really think we need ten pounds of butter?' As Jay succinctly pointed out, 'Well Robert, it's not like you can send the porters down for more sugar!'

Jay Smith had planned to visit Antarctica with the well-known mountain guide Mugs Stump and four clients, on an ascent of a new route on Mt Vinson. But Mugs had been one of the 11 people killed on McKinley earlier in the year when he fell into a crevasse. When Jay had called the four clients, they still wanted to go to Antarctica, as a memorial to Mugs. Jay decided to lead the trip, taking over where Mugs had left off, negotiating flights into the southern side of the mountain where no one had been before. This opened up the possibility of new routes and unclimbed peaks. I'd learned of Jay's plans and asked if he'd let Joe and me fly into the mountain with them. It was exciting, but also very risky. A few grainy photographs Mugs had of the area showed little, a 5,000-metre high mountain compressed onto a 5 x 7 inch print. Soloing into the unknown heights of the photographs was like a journey into space, climbing where no one had been before. And I had no experience of Antarctic conditions. But it was also an incredibly rare opportunity to solo a new route on one of the Seven Summits, something that couldn't be missed.

The trip to Antarctica started at JFK airport in New York, traversing the Atlantic, an endless sea of fluffy clouds leading into the early winter fog at Heathrow, the rain slanting sideways across the windows, the plane sending the spray wing-high as it hit the runway. A day later we were back from meetings in London, standing in the international terminal of Heathrow when the paging system echoed: 'Robert Anderson and Joseph Blackburn to customer service please.' Panic. Had we been dumped from the one flight that would connect with the flight to Antarctica? 'May I have your boarding passes, please?' I wasn't sure I wanted to give mine up, Antarctica melting in my dreams. 'Here you are, have a nice flight.' The new boarding passes were red, an upgrade to first class compliments of Peter Spencer, who was ensuring at least part of the Antarctic journey would be comfortable.

Stepping into the first class cabin was like being crowned a king for the 11-hour flight to Buenos Aires. Immense sleeper seats with tables that pulled out of the arms and swivelled, with room to walk around the front of them, food that rolled endlessly up and down the aisle, hot and cold entrées, chef salads prepared beside the table, fish lightly fried and served piping hot from the pan, a choice of vegetables running from baby potatoes to fresh asparagus, followed by fruit flan and chocolate cakes. The flight attendant, learning of our destination, pressed us to sample the desserts. 'At least two, certainly, gentlemen, I can't imagine you'll have many of these in Antarctica.' The climbing movie, *K-2,* was plugged into the video and the only thing missed was the chance to sleep. The feeling of luxury, of travelling in an era when air travel was a great adventure and the destination a remote and unexplored land, was too exciting to waste in sleep, no matter how much goose down was in the pillows.

Buenos Aires came and went, then the plane crested the Andes, Aconcagua hovering high above the range, the Polish Glacier and South East Ridge jutting high above the clouds, as clear as if my footprints still extended along the ridge and onto the top of South America where I'd stood nine months before. The heat of Chile wafted through the door of the plane as it opened on the Santiago summer. As the sun set, the next flight floated south, hugging the coastline, blue sea circling dark island peaks, clouds building up over the land, circling in and out of the fjords reaching in from the sea. The clouds were like pink candyfloss in the fading light against the deep green of the mountains; further south the rock and ice of Patagonia glowed dully in the dark, patches of ice standing out like sparks against the darkness of the rock. It felt like the bottom of the earth should have been reached and passed long ago.

Puenta Arenas was dark and quiet, a village set on the edge of the Straits of Magellan, our hotel just off the tree-filled square. The hotel was family run, like a Spanish pension, the kids dragging the bags up two flights of stairs and into a large room with three single beds, one for each of us and one, as the bellboy pointed out, for the stacks of luggage. While bodily we had made it to the southern tip of South America, the mind was still wandering around at the equator, the night's dreams flitting from winter to summer, seasons from autumn to spring, before a windy sunlit day dawned in Puenta Arenas.

Puenta Arenas is a fishing village and port built along a wind-swept hill, the tallest building just a few stories high. Wide streets with low curbs accentuated the feeling of a ghost town and cars strayed from side to side of the road with little regard for the dust-covered centreline. The houses were low and compact, thick wooden walls fitted with small-pane windows, lying in wait for another of the perpetual storms to blow in. At the grocery store with its Spanish packaging, it was back to shopping by pictures, but the large round sausages, squares of European cheese, elephant garlic and freshly ground coffee were essentials that could be located by smell alone, and the key to augmenting the well-stocked Antarctic larder. With a month on the ice planned, this was the only one of the Seven Summits where weight and conditions had reduced the menu to dried food, a few pre-packed noodles and sauces slid in around the edge of the pancake mix.

The food laid out on the floor back at the hotel stood in long stacks, row after row of butter, litre jugs full of olive oil, a bag of rice and another of potatoes, looking far more than seemed practical. Then counting the 28 days it had to last, doubts set in and memories of Scott's starving to death on the ice 18 kilometres from resupply surfaced. What if it wasn't enough? What if careful calculations were too conservative and the cold ate through the calories faster than planned? What if it all fell in a crevasse? The food was split into meals, then into weeks, then divided onto sleds, no one item packed in only one place, a hydra-headed insurance policy against our fears, food spread around as Hansel and Gretel did on their way through the forest. At least there were no fears of anything else eating the crumbs — the interior of Antarctica didn't even support a fly.

CHAPTER 24

PERILS OF PATAGONIA

THE AIRPORT WAS 20 kilometres north of Puenta Arenas and, after that, a single lane of concrete, one car wide, provided a smooth drive as long as no one was coming the other way. The problem was, there was so little traffic that it was easy to forget there was only one lane. After cruising along the dead flat road admiring the Straits of Magellan on one side and the fields of flowers and thick grass on the other, looking up would suddenly reveal an immense transport truck bearing down dead ahead, firmly fixed in the centre of the single lane. Brakes to the floor, hard swerve to the right, the car would lurch into the gravel, spitting stones in all directions, the truck would rush past with a burst of wind, then the front wheels clawed back up onto the cement, the back end of the car skewing into place and the journey continuing.

Perched alongside the road was a white two-storey hotel, veranda opening off the front, a hall set down the centre behind the screen door, bar opening off to the right, dining room to the left. Square tables, hard-backed wooden chairs and gingham checked tableclothes, tiny vase with flower in place, were straight from days gone by. Black and white photos lining the hall showed vaqueros seated on their sturdy ponies, lined up next to a herd of long-horned steers. The wild west was still alive and well in Patagonia. A small woman who doubled as the cook served up steak sandwiches, the meat flowing tender and juicy off the fresh sesame buns, set between fat slices of tomato and a stack of lettuce leaves.

The next day the luxury of the single paved lane was left behind, the road reduced to a gravel strip leading north into the Torres del Paine national park. The earth began to roll and twist as it left the plains. Huge fields opened up between the hills, lush with thick grass and covered with yellow flowers. Cow ponies grazed up to their waists in the grass, wading through the deep green as if at sea. Low clouds in the distance slid down over the granite spires of the Paine. The towers, granite carved smooth and towering over 1,000 metres in the air, were a climber's heaven, except for the storms that frequently swept out of the southern ocean and plastered them with ice. The soaring grey and black-streaked rock looked unearthly the closer the road got, lakes set in deep blue below, glaciers curving down out of the heights, tower after tower rising into the sky. The road twisted and curved and suddenly around a corner stood a large hairy beast. It looked like a cross between a tall, skinny and very hirsute horse and a small giraffe, deep sandy brown in colour, regarding us with large liquid eyes, unmoving and unafraid. After searching the hills of Aconcagua, it seemed all the guanacos had moved south. Like the animals of Africa, seeing it in the wild made it come alive and belong somewhere, instead of peering at it through the bars of a zoo. Around the corner was a small herd, the babies frolicking and curious, the mothers looking over their shoulders apprehensively. In the park they were protected and roamed wild, a hidden surprise in the depths of Patagonia.

On the return to Puenta Arenas the next day, the colours of Patagonia stood out strongly in the sunlight, the subtle hues of deep green grass and brown scrub, the muted milkiness of the glacial-fed lakes next to the deep blue of the spring-fed pools and the pure blue of the sky, cleansed by the ocean winds crossing the narrow southern tip of the continent. In the breeze was the hint of ice, with Antarctica and the icebergs of the southern ocean lurking just over the horizon.

Jay Smith and fellow guide Conrad Anker had arrived, packing food for their four clients. I'd first climbed with Jay on a summit bid on the West Ridge Direct on Mt Everest in 1985 and again on

Everest's North Face in 1990. A full-time guide and mountaineer, Jay had successfully blended his passion for climbing with his business, training the élite US Navy Seals in climbing techniques when he wasn't guiding private clients or off on his own expeditions. A day later, a group from the United Kingdom arrived, led by well-known British mountaineer Doug Scott and Roger Meare, who had skied to the South Pole several years previously on an expedition tracing Scott's epic journey.

Anne Kershaw, President of Adventure Network, who ran the DC-6 flight to Antarctica, briefed us on the procedure that afternoon. 'You'll need to wear your Antarctic gear, just in case the plane has to put down anywhere. Excess luggage is US$30 per pound. I don't mind if you have extra, but you'll have to pay for it, and besides, I may want to buy a new outfit so the more you have the better for me.' Blending business acumen with a dose of charmingly feminine capitalism, Anne had successfully guided the business since the death of her husband Giles Kershaw in a gyrocopter accident several years previously. 'The plane may leave later tonight, it may leave tomorrow, it may not leave for several days,' Anne added.

As the only private service flying to Antarctica, Adventure Network wanted to avoid any accidents that would require rescue by the government services who would have preferred they didn't fly there at all. They carefully monitored the weather for the eight-hour flight that would take us over Cape Horn, the southern ocean, along the Antarctic Peninsula and into Antarctica's interior, landing on a solid blue ice runway blown clean of snow. That night the weather at Puenta Arenas and the ice runway was good, but over the ocean gale-force winds blew and the flight was cancelled. Luckily, Puenta Arenas had streets full of good restaurants, fresh fish lightly fried in garlic, thick steaks, plates full of fresh vegetables and salads slathered with Italian dressing. Climbing stories spilled out of some of the best storytellers in the business, helped by Chilean wine and an underlying tension. 'We are off to Antarctica, soon.' An evening later dinner was interrupted with a shout. 'The bus will pick you up in two hours, be at the door with your bags.'

The shower barely dribbled as I stepped under it, everyone else in the hotel having the same idea, enjoying their last dose of soothing hot water before the departure for the showerless south. Long underwear, wind pants, double boots and furry ruffed coats came out. The front of the hotel on a warm spring day sprouted Antarctic adventurers sniffing the air for a cool breeze, sweating quietly and looking distinctly uncomfortable in the evening heat.

Doctor Sherman joined us, dressed in woolly shirt, heavy wool pants and insulated hunting boots. 'This is my third try to get to Antarctica. Two years ago the plane broke. Last year I tried and the weather delayed the flight two weeks and I had to go home. Maybe this year I'm lucky. The only good thing is, Anne Kershaw lets me fly at the original ticket price.' Doctor Sherman was from New York, had read every book worth reading on Antarctica and was bubbling with enthusiasm that he might finally set foot on the continent. We couldn't decide whether he was a good omen and he'd be third time lucky, or a jinx.

The bus swung into the airport next to the DC-6. It wasn't an inspiring sight. The plane was older than I was, but didn't seem to have aged quite as well. Rescued from a military plane graveyard, it had been fixed up, bolted together and put back into service. 'Ice Lady II' was lettered on the nose, immediately begging the question, 'Where was Ice Lady I?' One engine had been rewelded to the wing, coloured welding beads zig-zagging sporadically out across the wing. Entrance was up a steep and creaking ladder, hauling on a thick rope. Inside it was a dark metallic blue-brown shell. Lights were low, the floor was black and overhead rings were set military style into the ceiling. The seats looked like they may have come from a train, vintage 1950. But it was homely and it was going to Antarctica.

Halfway up the plane, a thin plywood panel with a rickety door led forward. Mounted on each side of the aisle were two shining steel auxiliary petrol tanks holding 520 gallons of fuel each. They were waist high and extended all the way forward to just behind the cockpit. The 16 hour round-trip flight required more fuel than could be carried conventionally, so the plane had been modified to fly the long distance down to and back from Antarctica without refuelling. Riding along behind the fuel was like riding a flying bomb. The huge props whirred to life, the co-pilot/flight engineer/ flight attendant stepped back to the doorway and said in a gruff voice, 'Put on your seat-belts, we'll be taking off now,' and disappeared. The plane loped slowly down the runway and rose so slowly into the air it hardly felt like it had left the ground. Terra del Fuego, strips of dark water and forest-clad islands, passed below. From an ice chest in the back of the plane, loaves of bread, slices of meat, apples and oranges were pulled out and we made sandwiches, sipping Cokes in the wash of heat flowing from the engines. Antarctic clothing was shed and the 25 passengers wandered about in long underwear, peering out the windows and snacking as we passed over Cape Horn, the final curve of South America disappearing below the plane.

Darkness fell and we dozed in our seats. When it was nearly dark it started to lighten again as the plane flew into the perpetual daylight of an Antarctic summer. The porthole windows looked out on black sea and stark white ice-floes, like an incomplete jigsaw puzzle set on the waves. The engines purred along with a confident roar, but ice began building around the windows, frosty fingers linking across the thin glass. The black water between the ice faded, to be replaced by endless ice, the white surface shining in the rising sunshine at 3 a.m. Breakfast was another sandwich at the cooler, then the plane started its slow descent towards the endless white below, pure flat ice extending to the horizon.

The DC-6 came in low over a few tiny orange tents, Patriot Hills, the seasonal Antarctic base for Adventure Network. The blue ice runway, which sounded like a simple idea, was a swath of just that, solid ice, heavily rippled in the crosswinds that created it. The co-pilot poked his head through the door as the plane skewed sideways in the wind, tipping like a yacht at sea. 'I don't suppose I need to remind you to put your seat-belts on?'

The plane hit the ground like it had been dropped straight onto the ice, smashing down with such force it hurt, sliding along, the pilot feathering the outside engines to steer, the co-pilot reversing the inside engines to slow our speed as we slid along with an eerie feeling of drifting helplessly on the ice. Finally it stopped. No one jumped up; we were frightened, the landing, the ice, the wind were too much all at once. Slowly a few people moved, the door was opened, a blast of ice-filled air flooded the cabin. The props spun to a halt and were silent. Across the ice, a snowmobile approached; the heavily masked driver and machine trailing smoke were like something from a Star Wars movie. There still wasn't a rush for the door, everyone putting on another mitten, then taking it off to relace their boots, then putting it on again.

The last step off the steep ladder was like a step onto the moon. The ice was solid, deep blue, heavily rippled, waves frozen in place, like a choppy sea. Everyone was walking around as though on eggshells. The last thing any of us mountaineers wanted to do was slip and fall over in front of our peers. The runway was set against a range of low mountains, snow covered with rocky ridges leading up them. To the north was the Patriot Hill camp, set in the midst of a vast ice sheet extending towards the horizon and the endless sea of white. Walking like penguins over the ice, we set out on the two-kilometre hike, slipping and sliding along. It was 6 a.m. after a sleepless night and Antarctica was a crystal dream, with coyote fur ruff whisping across the face for the first time, forming a tunnel of warm air to hide in, but smelling like a wet dog in its newness.

The long orange tent was 5 metres wide and 20 metres long, curving up in a half circle, like a pipe running half-submerged through the ice. Through the double doors, tables were lined up, sticking out from the wall. From the far end, steam rose from the kitchen. 'Would you like a cup of coffee?' A woman handed me a huge cup, steaming up my glasses, the perfect introduction to Antarctic hospitality. 'Did I really look like I needed a cup that bad?' I wondered gratefully. Bowls of soup followed and I remembered halfway through that this was breakfast, already sliding into Ant-

179

arctic time where things happened to suit mood, not the clock.

From Patriot Hills, we'd be taking a small Twin Otter plane for just over an hour west into the Sentinel Range where Mt Vinson was located. The wind was curving over the tents and whistling through camp, but Brydon the pilot, a veteran of many seasons of Antarctic flying, loaded us onto the plane with a laugh. 'We don't know where you want to go so how do we know what it's like until we get there? We'll just go fly around and have a look.' The Twin Otter, engines throbbing just outside the window, took off, skis spewing snow over the windows before the plane broke free into the air. Camp shrunk to a dot of orange immediately, swallowed by the whiteness.

Mountains jutted up as if growing from the ice. The world was ice, glaciers and mountains with the sun revolving endlessly around the rim of the earth. On the dash of the plane, a large sextant hung in front of the pilots, looking antique against the instruments flickering on the panel, but still the most reliable form of navigation in the changing atmospherics and magnetic fields surrounding the Pole. Brydon spread out a map. 'Now where is it you want to go, anyway?' Jay, Conrad and I peered over his shoulder, wavy lines of the topographical map bobbing about as the plane hopped through some turbulence. 'There, or maybe there,' said Jay, finger pointing below the southern reaches of Vinson. 'I'll have to make a pass to check for crevasses and wind, but that should be okay,' said Brydon. 'Don't know till we get there.'

The plane flew over the ice, glaciers rolling off the cliffs and down immense icefalls. Everywhere there was ice and more ice. Out the front window the Sentinel Range appeared, floating in the clouds, then Vinson became more distinct. We were flying at about 3,000 metres and the peak stood out far above us. It was suddenly apparent why it was called a massif. Rising from the glacier at little more than 1,000 metres, the ridges and faces climbed forever into the sky, kilometre after kilometre of mountain, with a summit plateau 3 kilometres long and 2 kilometres wide. The ridges stood out as jagged black flutes of rock and huge faces dropped 3,000 metres into the glaciers below. The plane swung low up the Nimitz Glacier, past the unclimbed Mt Craddock and its immense South Face, and nosed towards the snow. The light was so flat, the plane kept descending through layer after layer of white until the skis actually touched, then the powder snow swirled up around the windows, like skiing through drifts of deep powder. We stepped down into the untracked wilderness, 10 centimetres of pure snow, untouched and untrodden throughout history. The duffles landed with a thump. 'See you in a month, have a good climb,' waved Brydon and the Twin Otter powered down the hill, into the sky and was gone, leaving an emptiness, eight people and a stack of gear looking far smaller than what any self-respecting person would expect to live on for a month.

To ward off the incredible loneliness, we started digging and chopping, cutting out snow blocks, stacking them up in a circle, dropping the tents into holes, the ice walls stacked as high as the roof line to ward off any Antarctic blasts. There wasn't a storm in sight, a light breeze wafted past, the temperature was a temperate ten below Celsius and the sun wouldn't go down for three months, but the calm was eerie, a silence so quiet it hummed. The stove roared to life in the alcove outside the front door, Antarctic ice melted in the pot, a bowl of clam chowder bubbled away, the last traces of civilisation faded as the loaf of fresh bread was sliced and apples pared. There was no telling if it was day or night, but the last horizontal sleep was a continent away. An air pad and a foam pad between us and the ice below, it shifted nonetheless with a crack, just to remind us that in Antarctica, 'life's a glacier'.

Dreams were from far away, in the warm land. All the other continents of the world had people, restaurants and cultures. Antarctica had none of this. Its personality was devoid of humanity or the atmosphere people lend to a land. It was ice and snow and wind, the sun perched perennially on top of the white expanse. It wasn't necessarily hostile, but waking up and looking out of the tent the first morning, it was empty of life and colour. It would be weeks before the absence of life highlighted how many shades of white there were. It was the only continent whose personality wasn't connected to people, but to the earth itself.

Three of Jay's four clients were from Texas, an enthusiastic group of men all with a wicked sense of humour. Steve Plumb, the consummate storyteller of the bunch, wandered past our tent. 'The only way to stay warm is to keep telling yourself you're warm, you're warm. Just try it, it works.' The sun on the tent was surprisingly hot, but the pan frozen solid from the night before, the tooth paste hardened in its tube and the fuel bottles filled with iced petrol, causing instant frostbite if spilled on the skin, were reminders that the ground rules had changed. The continent was now in charge of how life was conducted; we simply played along. Vinson towered huge and distant at the head of the glacier.

With the loads packed tight, Joe and I roped up and started the long walk, sleds dragging along behind like errant schoolkids, never quite knowing which way to go. Entering the valley leading to Vinson, white became more and more dominant, the only note in the palette of the sky and the earth, as if colour had never been invented. The silent world was filled with new sounds, discovered hiding in the snow. Footprints squeaked through the powder snow, then thudded onto the ice below. Crevasses echoed hollowly underfoot. Ski poles probed the snow like sensors, indicating depth, how far the feet would sink, testing for crevasses hidden under the surface. While we were walking, the temperature was comfortably warm. On stopping, the breeze iced the body in seconds. A forearm in the sun was sunburned in minutes, a forearm in the shade had frost on it. On other peaks it had been cold, but perhaps for a day or two, not incessantly. In Antarctica, life was cold, full stop. Simple mistakes — a broken stove, twisting an ankle, letting a mitten blow away or a rip in the tent — would quickly unleash a wave of problems.

CHAPTER 25

THE SUNSHINE FACE

I'D WANTED TO CLIMB an easy route on Vinson to start with, something that allowed me to get used to the ice, the loneliness and the biting winds. But as we'd ascended the glacier towards the peak, the South Face of Vinson had revealed itself. In the centre was a sweeping line of ice, cutting through the rock like a long arc of curving ski tracks. It led up the entire 2,000-metre high face to where it pinched off, a thin ice runnel leading to the top. It was a natural line, one that in the Alps would have rapidly become a classic. But here, no one had seen it before, let alone contemplated climbing it. I assured myself I could always come down if the climbing became too difficult, while knowing that is often easier said than done.

Joe departed with Jay's party to video their ascent and camp was suddenly very empty, a spare tent flapping in the wind. They would be away for five days. For some reason, days had flipped into nights and at 7.30 a.m., dinner finished, I went to sleep for the day. The sun revolved around us and I was up again in the afternoon. While updating my diary, the pen froze. Perhaps it needed its own sleeping bag?

Above camp, a long ridge shot out from the side of Vinson, into the subsidiary peak, Mt Slaughter, providing a warm-up to Vinson while giving a better view of the face. Following the glacier up and around led to below the ridge, then straight up the ice, over the rock, which was surprisingly solid, reddish brown and in large chunks, cut with dark stripes, but with no moss or lichen like that found high on other peaks. At the ridge, the view spread out into the far valley, over further ridges and out past the Base Camp, across the Nimitz Glacier, up into a lower range of mountains, then off into a huge ice plateau disappearing south into a hazy never-never land. Looking back, I saw the South Face of Vinson bathed in sunshine, the route appearing in a different perspective. It was less steep at the bottom and steeper at the top than it had looked front on. Comparing the ridge elevation to the map, I realised the two kilometres of vertical now towered in its true light, clouds swirling about the ribs of rock jutting into the sky far overhead. There was no escape high on the face to anything easier, it would be either up to the summit or down in failure if it proved too hard. And with the hardest part at the very top, it would be a very long, difficult climb to fail on and have to retreat from. Since I would be carrying no ropes, rappelling out of any difficulties wouldn't be possible; only climbing down would provide an escape. But the only way to know if the route was actually achievable was to climb up and have a look.

Back in camp, water melted straight from the ice had a clean fresh taste that filtered slowly through the South American coffee, a brew the finest coffee shop would have been proud of. The batteries, warmed in a sleeping bag, powered the Walkman speakers with a sound that resounded from the back of the tent. Eighteen hours on the ridge had passed quickly with no fatigue, no frostbite and fewer fears of the great unknown hovering outside the tent door. It still seemed like soon the sun should be setting, but it would only go so far as to dip marginally in the south, riding along high over the ice, still a good 30 degrees above the horizon at 2 a.m. There was more darkness when a cloud passed over the sun than in the hours of night. Sleep, which should logically have been difficult, was deep and dream-filled. The world was eating and drinking, sleeping and climbing, with the body clock set by activity and, unexpectedly, the body seemed to like it. It was the first time the 24-hour hand on my Rolex, normally set to indicate time in a different zone, was used to tell whether it was night or day.

Clouds laced the sky overhead, patchy with streamers trailing out behind, unrelated to the wind below, travelling over the ice with a mind of their own. At midnight a star-burst formed around the sun, a parhelion with four suns set around the central and only real sun, connected by a string of light, like a single-stranded rainbow, hovering above the ice like a spaceship. A Stephen Venables recipe from Everest, a hint of lemon, sliced sun-dried tomatoes and black olives cooled in the tabbouleh while the rice pilaf bubbled on the stove. Suffering was about to commence but, until then, the Antarctic Café was open on demand.

Mist and cloud wreathed the peaks the next day, or was it night? More food and sleep, resting for the peak. The summit was over 2,000 metres above, then a very long traverse across the summit plateau at over 5,000 metres, not a good place to get tired. The sun-cream had now joined the toothpaste in its frozen state, the butter was a brick best removed with the ice axe, soap was brittle and flaky, the olive oil had turned to sludge. The only thing still liquid in the food bag was a carefully decanted bottle of Glenfiddich single malt whisky in a plastic waterbottle. Maybe it was a sign we should have brought more? The warning 'refrigerate after opening' on some of the food packs was the easiest direction to follow with life going on in an ice-box.

Porridge, laden with honey chopped from the bottle in squares, was a late-afternoon breakfast. Light inner socks, thick outer socks, foam inner boots, plastic outer boots, foam over-boots and then crampons were clicked on. Why did going out for a climb feel like going to war? Senses were heightened; the warmth of the tent washed around like a haven against the world outside. On my head went the Alaskan souvenir, the beaver fur hat, ruff pulled forward around the face, with a frost-free warmth and softness no miracle modern fabric could match. Outside the tent, a ski pole in one hand, ice axe in the other, I felt like the last man on earth. Why climb this thing anyway? There wasn't a whole lot else to do here though, it was mountains or nothing. Maybe I'd just go and have a look? The more I looked at the face, the more foolish it seemed.

The slope led slowly upwards across the glacier, then the face grew abruptly steeper. With the bergschrund crossed, a vertical hop from glacier to mountain, the flats below were left for the mountain above. The line of ice was a slanted ramp, a natural highway through the black rock. The higher it went, the better the ice became. The ramp thinned into a narrow gully, then nipped down to solid ice between the rock, just under vertical. The ice was blue, the front points bit cleanly, the axes followed, as solid as the continent below. The climb was so consuming that the top of the face finished abruptly. The acres of steep rock and ice that fell away below were part of a dream. The actual summit was still a 3-kilometre hike over false summits, an airless walk, crampons skittering across black ice.

Somewhere on the summit plateau I took a wrong turn, mistaking one bump for another. The compass spun uselessly and the map was too large a scale to have even half the 100-metre bumps that dotted the plateau on it. Wandering aimlessly, by a process of elimination I finally deduced that one bump was bigger than the rest, the furthest one away. Twenty hours out of camp, sandwiches and water exhausted, a final hidden ridge led to the top of Antarctica. The wind cut through the clothing like I was naked. The ridge was suspended between opposite sides of the peak, both falling away into the high plateau, like riding a wave set high in the sky above the ocean-white of the continent. A single upended ski pole marked the summit. Fifteen minutes on top reduced me to a shivering ball of ice. There was no time to think of enjoying the view. The cold felt dangerous, the view froze on my memory, the Sentinel Range set in a different reality atop the continent, then I turned and headed down before I became a part of it.

The climb down warmed me to marginally freezing. The descent wound out across the plateau, through the wide glacier leading out to the pass extending over to Mt Craddock, then a quick drop down the icefall and back below the South Face, looking up at my footprints still fresh on the ice above. Thirty hours after leaving the tent, I crawled back through the door.

Silent, so silent. Jay's party was still on the hill for another couple of days, moving up from camp to camp and then down again. While washing my hair in the warmth of the tent I had the bright idea to dry it quickly in the breeze outside. The hair seemed to dry immediately, then I realised it had frozen, iced over; the wind was an instant ice cube maker.

Jay and his party arrived back dejected, lost like me on the summit plateau, but frostbite setting in before they could sneak the final few feet up the ridge to the top. Two of the party would fly out in a few days; Jay, Conrad, Paul and Clive would move towards the tallest unclimbed peak in Antarctica, Mt Craddock, while Joe and I curved across the valley to the base of Mt Atkinson. The unknown in making a first ascent, the feeling of treading virgin ground with surprises just around the corner, makes ascending unclimbed mountains like finding diamonds in the ice. The North Face of Atkinson was a straight run to the summit, the day warm and welcoming, lunch on top a picnic. A day later, a second peak finished up as a thin ridge perched high above the Nimitz Glacier, an easy climb but a spectacular position. Just for good measure, the actual summit was three metres of shattered rock jutting straight up. Joe belayed me in case the whole thing toppled over and I clambered up, crampons scratching, fingers freed from the gloves, with a final pull up over the lip and onto the tiny summit, a first and last ascent of Mt Mads, probably for a very long time. The pale blue ice rolled off into the white and the sky. The mountains rose like pyramids with distinct personalities, each shooting out of the ice in a different pattern. The expanse of white below looked larger than a single earth should be. The glacier beneath us was indistinguishable between ice and cloud, so softly did the light fall.

CHAPTER 26

THE ROLEX RIDGE

At Base Camp where the plane had dropped us off, the reserve food bags held the flash-frozen tuna, the parmesan cheese, the sun-dried tomatoes, the elephant garlic, the extra litre of olive oil and a sip of single malt to welcome us back to civilisation. The sleds were left in a heap, tent slotted into the igloo walls we'd built on landing, as if we'd never left. Joe had been dragging enough camera equipment to make a Hollywood movie and the nerves in his hip had been shooting pains through his leg from the sled harness. An extra whisky and a day's rest was prescribed. The cold had cracked the metal on the stove, which had taken to fizzing and flaring on start-up. Joe's ability to fix anything with few tools came in handy, a talent adapted from days underwater working on the electrical systems of nuclear submarines, another place where you can't just nip out for a spare part. New gaskets and a jury-rigged valve later, the stove roared back to life and the pancakes flowed off the pan like a fast-food kitchen, maple syrup melted into frothy crystals and ladled over the top.

Vinson still loomed in the background, dwarfing all around it. The plane was due in four days, barely time enough for one more climb if everything went perfectly. The day started with the bristles falling out of the toothbrush into my mouth, too many extremes of heat and cold stressing the different plastics of the bristles and the handle.

The West Face of Vinson had always been the primary goal ever since the first view of the mountain. It rose over 3,000 metres, a single sweep from the base to the summit plateau that had never seen a footstep. A single ridge framed its right side, separating the West from the South West Face. I'd already named it the Rolex Ridge; all it lacked now was an ascent.

Having never ascended 3,000 metres of vertical in a single push before, getting up and down in a day had a lot of question marks attached to it. While it was certainly possible on established routes or where the chance of escape existed, attempting a new route in the depths of Antarctica could well turn me into a snowman before I finished. Turning back early was always a possibility, but climbing with no sleeping bag, tent or stove, if I stopped, any problems would be quickly solved when I froze. The supply of chocolate, crackers and water were only designed to keep me moving.

We moved camp higher under leaden skies, wandering up an unexplored glacier through an immense icefall, threading glaciers and feeling smaller and smaller the closer to the mountain we got. The valley had never been explored before though, and while the slog through the snow was less then exciting, the feeling of treading new ground, seeing vistas never seen before, kept the eyes wide, like children on a school holiday. In the centre of the valley, a hidden crevasse opened up, its lip dipping exactly a tent-level deep, providing the perfect camp site, protected from the elements.

After sleeping through the day, a voluminous dinner feast of fettuccine bubbled over the sides of the pot before there was even a chance to wake up properly. At midnight I left the tent, timing the ascent to be on the summit plateau during the marginally warmer midday hours. The sun hid above a pack of low clouds that obscured the peak. The tent receded below quickly, a tiny dot in the centre of the huge white expanse. The light was so flat only my crampons defined the ups and downs of the glacier. The hanging valley, without a human footstep, floated airily, suspended between the ridges that rose into the clouds overhead.

The route led up onto the ridge. Drifted snow cut away underfoot, the first avalanches slid away in swaths. Hanging ice towers loomed overhead. I threaded through them, sneaking around their heights, the second ice tool coming out as the final cliff loomed below the ridge. A front point, ice-tool dance led to the crest of the ridge. Mist rose up in a flat floor underfoot, the sun shooting across its surface, the clouds spread before me as if the snow floated straight out into the clouds. The ridge stretched above, the ice, the snow and the rock in endless patterns. Ice crystals were set in the rock since the beginning of time, crystals so big they were like miniature hands in the snow, their fingers a million filigrees of white, the sun reflected through them like glass. I felt a trespasser climbing through them.

The ridge loomed ominously as my mind worked on a section at a time, a footstep at a time. The halfway point came and went, the ridge looked as far above now as below, both distances too far to think about. My legs ground along as if on an endless treadmill. How many footsteps in three kilometres of vertical? Ice cliffs rose out of the face, unseen from below and towering large in reality. Real climbing was required, ice going black, the ice tools bouncing on ice like it was steel, with a detour back onto rock, steep but exhilarating, air falling away below. Fatigue brought questions. Would the body keep taking these endless steps? The scale was too large to think about, the mind creeping off to see the body alone on the face, ant-like but slower, sitting, waiting to see if it would keep moving. The ridge slid out onto the summit plateau and wind swept the snow in rivers over the ice. The cold was frightening, just a change of jacket had to be thought out to the last move. Pack off, outer mittens off, pack open, climb 100 metres to warm up, jacket out and on, mittens on, the fingers burning with cold, pack on, walking, the crampons skittering on the brick-hard ice. Don't stop, don't pause, don't freeze. It was all so simple.

The final summit pyramid loomed in a wave of cloud, an angry grey monster whipping over the highest exposed point on the continent. At least this time I knew where the top was. The summit ridge boiled in ice 150 metres above. The only alternative was a steep face leading directly to the top. Failure was whipping in the wind. Movement calmed the fears, the familiar pattern of the ice tools swinging, ice flying, points leading the feet towards the summit. A rock flew through the air overhead, torn from the ridge. The summit loomed and approached, the body moving automatically. A final footstep, a seat a foot wide on the top of Antarctica, the cold setting in immediately, the wind dying completely, leaving a vacuum of cold air that felt colder than the wind. The top: the continent stretched out below, the world's loneliest continent, the highest point, no sign of humanity in sight. The mountains marched in single file to east and west. Far out on the horizon, mini-peaks rose from the ice plateau, like shadows sailing in a sea of white, cruising with the winds. Clouds wreathed up the face below, throwing ice crystals heavenward.

The South Pole seemed visible over the horizon. The continent with no people had yielded up the best summit, the purest climb. I felt no longer myself, but a piece of humanity balanced against a continent without. I was just aware enough of my elevated condition to realise it was a very dangerous world, thoughts connected to the crampons on the ice, the ice axe at the ready. Automatically I turned and started down.

Thighs burned on the descent, the view looking down the face and across the glacier so far below it worse than the view coming up had been. The route became steeper with fatigue, every step placed on the ice demanding perfection, the possibility of steel-on-ice security being turned into a roller-skate ride in the changing conditions. Ice chunks broke loose and tumbled down the face, rolling and tumbling out to blow up on the glacier far below. The final descent to the glacier off the ridge was a leg-shaking endurance test, the points of the feet kicking feebly into the ice, every tool carefully set as a back-up to a body overstrung and overstretched.

Hallucinations crept into the white reality, climbers appeared around me, followed me down. The clouds hummed and bells rang from behind the rocks on the ridge. It had been too far for too long; part of me watched my body, part of me watched my mind at work, and there was another part keeping track of everything, a new part that hadn't been there before. I need this, I thought, I need a lot of looking after right now.

Waking from the depths of the sleeping bag, unable to remember the arrival at camp, the final descent of the face blending into dreams of the night, dreaming it was dark, waking to another endless day, the twenty-eighth day in Antarctica. The ice continent finally felt like home.

VII
ASIA

CHAPTER 27

HISTORICAL HORRORS

In 1985 I made my first trip to Everest with 19 people, stalling out at 8,500 metres when Jay Smith and I came to a halt in deep snow with oxygen bottles fizzing uselessly at our feet. In 1988 I was back with a team of four, without oxygen, Stephen Venables reaching the top on a new route up the Kangshung Face. Again I stopped short, this time at the South Summit, a mere 100 vertical metres shy of the top, probably little more than an hour away. With the wind whistling like a thousand demons, blinded by the snow, and a 17-hour day above 8,000 metres behind me, I thought I might make the top, but knew I'd die trying to get down. So I retreated.

In 1990 I was back with a team of six during the monsoon, climbing up the Super Couloir towards the Hornbein on the North Face, a single push taking Mark Hesse, Harry Kent, Jay Smith and me from 5,800 metres to 7,600 metres, only to be met by a storm that dumped a metre of snow overnight, which miraculously didn't avalanche, and we slid back down the next day in several hours of glissading. As we had climbed without ropes or a tent, it suddenly seemed that perhaps a solo, something I'd always dreamed about, just might be possible. So six months later I was back, with only my partner Margaret Seddon to keep me company and Passang Nurbu, our Sherpa, in the kitchen. But the standard pre-monsoon season was too early and too cold to solo without oxygen.

The first attempt in early May came to a halt at 8,100 metres after a bivouac that frostbit my toes off while two ridges away a fellow soloist, Rudi Lang, decided to spend one more night and froze solid. The reasons for failure on Everest now ran: oxygen, too slow and storm, monsoon conditions and wrong season. I followed this with a quick expedition to the North Ridge where our large team wandered futiley around in blizzards and then was back the next year, just in time to greet a monsoon season that never stopped.

In all these attempts there had been a number of close calls, particularly in 1988 when Stephen Venables, Ed Webster and I spent four days crawling down from the South Col after running out of food and water. But in 1993, being very close to death was condensed into a few short hours, with the prospect of being buried alive growing by the minute. Mike Bearzi, Mike Duncan, Paul Teare and I climbed from Advanced Base to the High Camp at the base of the North Face, from where I would launch my solo ascent. That night it snowed from 9 p.m. until 4 a.m. when the first avalanche hit us.

The North Face of Everest rose 2,000 metres directly above camp, though a ten-metre wide, 100-metre deep crevasse just behind the tent and a kilometre of flat ground should have swallowed the avalanche. But, in the end, there was nothing to stop two square kilometres of snow two metres deep when it decided to fall straight down the face. A tent is a tomb when it is buried. The frozen nylon curled around my face and the snow packed around my body, enclosing it like shrink-wrapped meat. From a half-dead sleep, I felt the power of the snow smash into the tent, throwing me about with a terrifying violence. There was nothing to do but bash the walls out to save a breath of air, while I felt blindly for headlamp and glasses in the pitch black. Hunched like a crab I scuttled to the far end of the tent and ripped through the top of the door. It was snowing heavily, completely silent. The white was like a wall.

We had been in three small tents, one of which was still to my right, two metres away. But to the left, nothing. A clear swath marked where it had been. My sleep-filled mind stared at the place, as it willed the tent to reappear. Paul Teare and Mike Duncan had been in there, somewhere. The other tent held Mike Bearzi, who now poked his head out. One tent had disappeared, my tent was half gone and Bearzi's was fine. Voices like whispers called through the blizzard. Mike and Paul were there, just buried, sounding like gremlins muttering from under the snow.

In my tent everything was chaos, thrown about and half buried in the folds. Outside, the occasional roar of an avalanche still echoed through the dark. One avalanche didn't ensure there wouldn't be more. Camp was in a basin surrounded by mountains on three sides. The more it snowed, the more a death-trap the camp became.

I couldn't decide whether to dress for the blizzard or get out immediately and dig Paul and Mike out. While I laced my boots, they could well be suffocating. Settling for boots, long underwear and a big jacket I stepped out into the storm. It was snowing so hard the headlamp barely penetrated, then the snowflakes reflected back the beam like a car's approaching headlights. The snow was waist deep. Only a small circle of fabric poking from the surface marked Paul and Mike's tent. When the avalanche hit they'd made a tiny space, their faces smashed together just under the roof. They needed air. The only thing still sticking from the snow was a ski pole, the shorter ice axes buried in the snow. The first stab tore the tent's roof open and the second ripped into the tent itself. Snow poured in. Paul and Mike's eyes were big and they gulped air through the hole. Gratitude echoed from their tiny cave. Snow enveloped them to their shoulders, the tent crushed against them, snow holding them tight. If the snow had been any deeper or swept them with it, they would have been very hard to find.

The swath of the avalanche was a twisted river of ice that had obliterated everything before it. Bearzi and I dug for an hour to free them. The tent was gone, squashed, buried. Camp had shrunk to half my tent and Bearzi's smaller tent. We huddled drinking cold tea from a thermos. It was still snowing, still completely white outside. At 6 a.m. a feeble grey dawn broke through the storm. At 7 a.m. a larger-than-usual gunshot crack signalled another avalanche release. The roar that followed sounded like a thousand freight trains. A kilometre away, the ice wall of Everest's North Peak dropped from the sky. It was so far up and so far away it seemed improbable it would hit us. Bearzi, standing outside the tent, monitored it like a sports announcer. 'Looks okay so far, hard to tell, it's still coming, you better get ready. Oh no, it's definitely gonna get us.' The avalanche disappeared into a trough, then headed uphill towards camp, a wave of air blasting snow into a cloud 100 metres high. Fearing burial, I dived out the tent door. A chunk of ice the size of a bowling ball flew past my head like a comet and buried itself in the glacier. I dived back inside. The wave of air blasted through camp and the tongue of the avalanche took out the side of Bearzi's tent, flattening it like a burst balloon. The discussion was short and terse. Mike Duncan clarified the options. 'I don't care what we do, but I'd like to get out of here alive.' Mountain lore says that the worst avalanche danger is during or just after a storm. But all the rules had been broken. Camp at 6,500 metres, a 12-hour blizzard, avalanches burying camp from two directions. Escape was the only option.

A curious half-dawn still existed, snow dropping so thick it felt heavy in the air, like a torrential downpour. With skis on, sliding downhill was the only indication there was a hill sloping away from camp. Ice chunks the size of Volkswagens were only recognised when the skis rammed into them. The roaring continued and avalanches disappeared into crevasses hidden in the storm. Looking back, the only distinguishable feature was three ghostly figures following my tracks, like abominable snowmen emerging out of the mist. We skied down through the clouds, appearing on the glacier far below like angels, floating back into life with a laugh and long, swooping turns.

Advanced Base Camp had Passang in his kitchen, a tent called home, alpine grass, blue sheep, and a small flock of fat birds wandering from tent to tent pecking stones. Every night, 15 minutes of international news via Radio Nepal told of floods and 'the worst monsoon in 100 years'. The summer climbing season was nearly over, the storms sweeping through Advanced Base Camp with frightening irregularity. There was no pattern, just washes of snow and wind with never more than a day of sunshine, just enough to raise hopes, inspire a 7-hour, 1,000-vertical-metre climb back up the glacier, a fear-filled night in the relocated camp surrounded by avalanches, then a powder snow run back down the hill, dodging avalanches and snow-snakes as the weather closed in again.

By 10 September I'd given up. The permit was up in five days, yaks were scheduled for departure. I had only to clear camp at the base of the North Face. There would be no more of the interminable waiting, the hopes when the sun came out, the depressions when it snowed all night. If nothing else, two months in a tent would end. Not successfully, not really happily. But it would end and the privations of a 5,500-metre lifestyle would at last be over.

11 September, 1993, dawned clear. The 2 a.m. start for High Camp had become slightly more bearable with practice. I packed enough for the day and threw in an extra bag of dried potatoes and a bar of cheese, just in case the weather held. Frustration had settled so deep and hopes had been dashed so many times, that soloing Everest had faded back into my dreams. Paul Teare and Mike Bearzi skied up with me to clear their equipment from camp, packed and disappeared down the mountain. My one shred of desire allowed a last night up high. One day the 100-year monsoon had to stop and after two months waiting, I could only hope this would be it. If the weather held one night, I could at least attempt the peak. The nightmares of 1991, the ghosts wandering around camp and the privations of altitude, had all been battled into their corners. Dinner was staged to keep busy, keep demons and gremlins at bay, going from dessert, a Power Bar, to tea and sleep before the ghosts could get me.

Three a.m., 6,500 metres, a million stars overhead, no snow, no clouds, one final chance to climb to the top of the world. The stove sputtered to life, I sputtered to life. It was 200 metres of vertical and a kilometre to the North Face on skis. There wasn't a cloud in the sky or a person in sight. Soloing Everest was the loneliest job in the world. But for once the avalanches were quiet.

The North Face of Everest isn't steep enough to trouble a modern climber, nor gentle enough to let you off easily if you fall. Most soloists either fail so low they couldn't fall off, or get so high they can't get down.

The weather remained deceptively beautiful, but the month of snow had left the face a sloppy morass. If it were one type of snow there would be a rhythm to climbing. But the snow varied from hip-deep sugar to calf-deep crust. By 2 p.m. I'd reached 7,600 metres. A tiny tent buried from an earlier foray provided 12 hours of refuge, then I set off again. The Great Couloir, a shallow scoop leading towards the summit head-wall, led inexorably upwards. From Advanced Base Camp it had looked like a narrow gully. Inside, it was 200 metres wide and a kilometre high. Rough avalanche tracks had formed drifts and ice chunks made miniature mountains as every step became more laboured. After 12 hours' climbing, the Yellow Band, a near-vertical step of rock that extends from 8,300 to 8,400 metres, cut across the Couloir. Large expeditions have spent up to a day fixing ropes and pounding pitons on this section. I planned on clambering up it with some historical skills and a lot of luck. One thin rope dangled down the passage to show the way, but its frayed sheath dispelled any hopes for a safe ascent. I was forced onto the front points of my crampons and tucked my mittens inside my coat to grasp the rock with my bare fingers. I forgot I was at altitude and after several hard moves was left gasping for air every time I reached a thin ledge to balance on.

The Yellow Band was shattered and brittle and rocks peeled off in my hands to bounce down the face. Fifty metres up the rock I peered straight down between my legs and realised this was real climbing, where a fall would quickly place me amongst the angels. Another gasp for air, the rock turned to ice, frozen fingers were forced woodenly back into the gloves and ice axes back into position. I crouched on the ice, but the relief only let my body take over from my mind which had forced it too far. Nausea swept over me, my stomach cramped and threw up, retching bile into the snow. The pain became ugly, legs cramped, arms were wooden, the brain dulled. Climbing Everest hadn't turned out to be much fun.

The day crept on as I crawled towards the ridge. Snow had drifted into the Couloir. Where the snow should have hardened in the wind, it only deepened, until I was swimming uphill. I fought on for another hour, until a cold numbness crept in. Rocks beneath the snow caught and twisted the crampons and the sun went out behind the ridge. For two days my feet had been deep in the snow, the cold sucking them dry, the blood retreating. I hated frostbite, the numbness followed by the months of pain, the bloody blisters and hobbling around like a chicken.

At the ridge the snow lay in waves. It was 6 p.m. and the altimeter read 8,410 metres. Above, cliff bands had banked the snow up in drifts, rolling, waist-deep barriers of settled sugar snow. It was a quick, simple decision in the end. The snow would slow progress and it would take at least eight hours to reach the summit, maybe more. I could climb for two days without sleep, but probably not three. If I kept going and made it, it would be a failed suicide, not a success. I wanted to have at least some say in finally reaching the top, something besides knowing I was lucky. It was 6:15 p.m., time to fail quickly and make a valiant effort to get off the mountain alive.

From my position at the top of the rope, the Yellow Band disappeared below my feet, looking twice as steep and much bigger than on the climb up. I wrapped the rope around my arms in a rapid rappel technique suited to sea-level cliffs. It was a fast but extremely dangerous way to get down very quickly. The rope burned out through the mittens, crampons scraped, sparks flew and I was down, shivering, huddled in a ball on the steep ice slope. It was a terrible thing to have to push the body this far just to stay alive. It was retching and shivering and whimpering. The hallucinations started then, I felt them coming. Unlike previous expeditions where they crept up unannounced, my mind was familiar with them, it recognised them and they swept in all at once. Paul Teare, Mike Bearzi and Mike Duncan came back to climb down with me. A short woman who I never quite saw wanted me to go left. I had never dropped a mitten climbing, but I did. But it wasn't me that dropped it. My left and right hand belonged to different people and my left hand, now with only a thin glove on it, was getting colder and colder. The rest of me was kind enough to stop and warm it up. Night settled, the darkness turned pitch black and the footprints which cleared a path 18 hours before had disappeared into an avalanche fan. Camp should be somewhere, but with feeble starlight the snow was a white desert and the rocks were black forms dancing about on the snow. I waded through a hallucination of climbers, mountains, music and the left hand not knowing what the right hand was doing. The tiny tent at 7,600 metres was nowhere to be found. Dreams of the tent, a stove, a drink, a chance to warm my frozen toes rose up like a mirage. In the end life was a metre-deep snow cave tunnelled out with the ice axe. Boots came off and toes rested against calves in a vain attempt to get them above numb. I knew they were in trouble.

Dawn, head on my boots; spindrift avalanches filtered into the shallow cave in the ice. I was covered with a fine blanket of ice crystals. The body said it would quite happily die, barely having the energy to shiver, and when it did, violent spasms passed through my core. It was another 1,000 metres down the mountain to the camp of too many avalanches, 10 kilometres onto Advanced Base Camp and another day on to Base Camp. I was late, even the yaks had left me behind. I hadn't been to the top, but I would make it back down. And I'd finally had a climb, if not to the top at least a climb, which is what I wanted when I started out. The summit still waited as a final destination, the public finale. The personal experience completed the expedition for me. For 1993, at last, it was over, but not finished.

CHAPTER 28

THE DAY OF THE GORAK

EVEREST. BACK FOR THE THIRD attempt to solo the peak and the seventh visit overall. I had failed to reach the summit more times than anyone I knew, except, as Norbu Tenzing kept encouraging me, his father, Tenzing Norgay. But getting up the first time with Ed Hillary may have been just a bit more problematical than even a solo. While the journey to Everest had become familiar, the experiences were always so different. The only thing that remained the same was the ground covered, although since we travelled in the height of the monsoon it seemed to wash away with frightening regularity.

The traditional south side of Everest, which had first been ascended in 1953 by Hillary and Tenzing, now had people running up it with seasonal regularity. But this route would be a very treacherous solo through the crevasse-ridden Khumbu Icefall. The number of people, ladders, ropes and prepared camps also made it as removed from real climbing as one could get. Climbing with oxygen also takes away Everest's biggest challenge, the altitude, to the extent that modern climbing techniques defeat the purpose of climbing it in the first place. Lightweight titanium oxygen cylinders, costing US$500 each, carried to high camps by Sherpas and simply picked up and turned on by climbers, make it possible for virtually any relatively fit person to ascend the regular route on Everest.

To solo Everest, avoiding the icefall, the climb started from the opposite side of the mountain, which was both steeper and more difficult. Reading the record books, it was also hard to ignore that only one person had soloed Everest, Reinhold Messner, while at least four I knew of, several in the past few years, had died trying. And while a few Americans and one New Zealander had ascended Everest without oxygen, they climbed in the midst of others who had broken trail, used oxygen and prepared camps. Expeditions that climbed free from oxygen were rare in conception and even rarer in their success rate. While Everest summiters number well into the hundreds, successful oxygen-free expeditions can be counted on the fingers and those climbing without pre-set camps (alpine style) number only two successful attempts.

Organising an Everest expedition, even after the experience of completing one a year for four years, meant raising money, organising food and equipment and negotiating with the Chinese Mountaineering Association in Beijing for a permit and transport. So in 1995 I invited Mike Bearzi and Eric Winkleman to accompany me. They'd help look after food, equipment and the myriad of logistics in Nepal and Tibet. Passang Nurbu returned to co-ordinate the Tibetan yak drivers and cook for us.

Five duffle bags were packed with the equivalent of enough food for one person for a year, 40 litres of high-altitude stove fuel and 300 rolls of film. Compared to a standard Everest expedition it was nothing, but on the overweight baggage scales, it looked horrendous. Hitting the ground in Kathmandu, the transition from the West to the East was immediate: from stuffing duffles with hi-tech solar panels to power the Compaq, the last-minute press conference and rushing onto the plane, to suddenly exiting in a fairytale land running at a completely different speed, almost in reverse. Kathmandu — the Himalayas on the horizon, the hot breezes and pouring rain of the afternoon monsoons — there was no place like it on earth.

Passang Nurbu was at the airport to greet us. Red brick buildings five stories high leaned over the streets of Thamel, which ran red with mud every afternoon in the rain. Mike Bearzi went off shopping while I checked the truck to make sure that despite its third-world price it still looked like it could crawl up to the border, an eight-hour drive across the serrated ridges of Nepal and up the river valley to the border with China.

We started at 4 a.m., traversed the mud slides of Nepal, tyres sliding over single-lane roads slanted precariously towards the rivers below. Slipping and sliding up the muddy track, we were at the border for lunch, transferred the luggage to an antiquated Chinese truck and crawled straight up the side of a cliff to the Zhangmu hotel in Tibet. A few woebegone Tibetans wandered about, but the Chinese Army presence dominated, 18-year-old refugees on hardship posting, hating life and exercising their authority with a blatant dislike for Tibet and anyone who travelled through it. Our Chinese liaison officer and interpreter greeted us, to act as guides in practice, but to look over our shoulders in reality, collecting fees for our every move.

The jeep was away at dawn the next morning, the monsoon draining out of the air like a shower being turned off the higher we travelled. The Tibetan Plateau was 4,000 metres high, windy and arid, filled with earth tones of the rainbow, rocks layered through the hills in oranges, reds and browns. The green fields of barley, whitewashed houses, yak dung drying on the ramparts and prayer flags flying from the rooftops, dotted the brown hills — hills that rose up to over 5,000 metres.

Along the dusty road, Tibetan houses were low and solid, formed from earthen bricks and whitewashed. Passang wandered off in a roadside village at lunch and soon returned to invite us for tea. The house was smoky but comfortable; thick yak-wool rugs lined the seats and brass kettles filled the shelves, sign of the well-to-do household. The room slowly filled, people sneaking in to crowd around the doorway and regard us with large brown eyes. Above the fireplace, a worn black and white photo of the Dalai Lama, framed in fringed silk prayer shawls, peered down. Religion is an essential part of the Tibetan existence, evident in what they wear, eat and think, permeating their day-to-day life with a consistency of purpose. As the jeep roared off, a group stood on the hillside, with a peculiar angular stance, legs slightly bent, balanced forward, hands behind their backs, solid but fluid.

The Himalayas rolled past as peaks shimmered in the sunshine and glaciers cascaded, remote and seemingly very close at the same time, their snowfields shooting straight out of the sandy-brown plateau. The jeep driver popped in another Top 3 Chinese disco tape, turned up the volume, leaned back in his seat and feathered the wheel through his black leather gloves as the tail slid through the loose gravel. Barring a flat tyre, mud slide, rockfall, or fight at the checkpoint with the young Chinese Army recruits waving their AK47s, riding through Tibet was just like Route 66.

The jeep pulled into Xegar late in the afternoon. The hotel was located inside thick walls two metres high, shutting out the Tibetans, a fortress that could quickly be turned into a military stronghold should the tide ever turn against the Chinese. Rooms smelled stale and damp, the plumbing rarely worked, the food was inedible, but the views were spectacular, set as we were in the midst of a broad valley above the river. Eight kilometres away, the monastery sat at the bottom of the cliff dwelling. It rose up the ridge in a series of castle-like walls, to a pinpoint summit festooned with prayer flags. In 1988 I'd had my most memorable visit with Norbu Tenzing. Learning of Norbu's heritage, the monk took us aside for endless cups of Tibetan tea, a potent mix of which the strongest ingredient was rancid yak butter. From years of chanting prayers, the monks develop phenomenal memories. With Norbu's Tibetan language skills, the monk was able to relate stories and tales prior to our visit to the Kangshung Valley that were half history, half prophecy. The Tibetan attitude to life is unique, a quiet strength that transcended their hard life, a co-existence with their environment that sees them live in the harshest of climates with a minimum of possessions, forsaking physical comforts for spiritual knowledge, not a bad course of study before embarking on Everest.

The Xegar hotel offered two choices. Stay longer than a day and get sick as a dog from the food. Or go immediately to Base Camp having climbed from little over 1,000 metres to 5,000 metres in three days. At least at Base Camp we would be in the shadow of Everest and altitude effects would fade quickly.

The quick overnight stay with a pre-dawn start didn't really wake us up until the top of the Pang La Pass. From there, standing directly to the south, was Everest, looking exactly like the tallest peak in the world should look. The North Face jutted straight into the air through ridges and ramparts, snowfields and ice cliffs; the top shot right up into the white plume, pulling Everest into the heavens. The Pang La Pass was at 5,000 metres, the top of Everest 3,800 metres higher, dwarfing everything around it. It was a view that, weakened by altitude, thousands of kilometres of travel, and the sudden glaring reality of the peak, left me feeling weak and small. What with the beating of the avalanche against the tent that nearly buried me two years ago, the ice cliff Roger Marshall fell and died from, the rock where Rudi Lang decided to stay an extra night a few years ago and where he still sits, and the Couloir where Michael Parmentier was last seen, the history of soloists on Everest wasn't very inspirational. The problem with visiting Everest more than once was that the knowledge of how to reach the summit was balanced by an equal knowledge of the failures, the difficulties and the pure ugliness that crept up at altitude until it felt like it was robbing the brain. A good day on Everest was the best day on earth, but a bad day was a guaranteed day in hell.

The jeep dropped into a broad river valley, the road passing an ancient village of Tibetan forts, dzongs, that sprouted from alongside the road. Several hundred years old, they protected the villages in the past, towering structures made from hard earthen blocks that seemed to grow straight out of the earth itself. At times the road followed little more than the river bed, then it crossed a bridge and curved around and up over alpine pastures into the Rongbuk Valley. The valley was made famous during the British attempts in the 1920s, as they wandered up past the Rongbuk monastery and onto Everest. The hills soon grew into cliffs, while the road wove a precarious path along the river. White-capped peaks poked out from behind the cliffs, the air thinned, a breeze blew down from the glacier and at the end of a long sweeping corner, the North Face of Everest came into view, dominating the head of the valley. The jeep toiled up the hill, crossed a wide boulder-filled stream, bounced over the round granite rocks embedded in the sandy soil and swept onto the smooth moraine at the foot of the glacier.

Base Camp was windy and dusty, set at the bottom end of the glacier with morning breezes wafting down the valley and afternoon winds roaring up it. In the monsoon it is often deserted, making it a welcome change from the high season on Everest when hundreds may be coming and going. For the North Face it is little more than a way-station, where truck power is replaced by yak power for a move ten kilometres up the glacier to Advanced Base Camp, which would be home for two months. Five kilometres below camp is the Rongbuk Monastery, the world's highest. Twelve monks and nuns stay there year round, with a few goats, yaks, and the passing expeditions to assist their subsistence living. A few days later we wandered back down the trail, sitting for three hours in the eerie darkness of the prayer room, while monks chanted, the beat of a gong echoed off the wall, a pair of metre-long horns hummed deeply while the prayers to protect Everest climbers, soloists, ensure good weather and not freeze my toes off, were murmured to the gods in a mesmeric chant that could best be repeated as 'a-be-bop-a-boo-bop', chanted ad infinitum while the candles flickered, the incense smoked and the tone rose and fell in waves, building to a crescendo before we escaped back out into the sunshine, halos hovering over our heads.

Back at Base Camp, the yaks had arrived, six hardy beasts that would carry 60-kilogram loads up the hill to Advanced Base Camp. The yak-herders were wild men, born into a set of clothes they seemingly still wore, with large chunks of coral in their ears, layers of rough yak wool slung over their shoulders and drooping dark heavy pants held up with a wand of rainbow wool wound round their waist. Passang came into his own, speaking fluent Tibetan, negotiating load size and our time of departure. I'd learned many expeditions previously that the Tibetans worked to a different schedule and in a different way, which Passang understood and organised more efficiently than I ever could. The members of the Chinese Mountaineering Association, unable to speak Tibetan, were of no use, the Tibetans mistrusting them from the time they took over Tibet and carrying a deep-seated dislike for their presence.

Leaving Base Camp, with its wind, dust and connection to the outside world at the end of the road, was always welcome. The rough trail wandered out along the glacier, then disappeared immediately into a geography dominated by Everest. The trail hugged the side of the valley, the glacier, over a kilometre wide, extending across the valley floor. An hour above Base Camp, the East Rongbuk stream boiled down out of the hidden gorge leading to the North Col, scene of the original British attempts. The trail disappeared into slick grey granite footstones tumbled from the slopes of Everest. Leaping from stone to stone, water cascading in torrents underfoot, we crossed the gateway to the inner sanctum of Everest.

Advanced Base Camp was a patch of heaven on the edge of the glacier. It was hard to imagine a more comfortable — and spectacular — setting. Located on a grassy terrace 100 metres above the Central Rongbuk Glacier, small lakes reflected the Himalayas and lush grassy tussocks framed small blue alpine pools. The camp was tight against the hill, so the winds whistled overhead, but rarely through camp. Days were sunny and warm, the tents heating up to 30 degrees Celsius inside. Nights dropped below freezing but a cup of tea, delivered to the tent door in the morning as the sun hit, quickly warmed the spirits. If waiting for the weather of the monsoon to provide a window of opportunity was frustrating, conditions at Advanced Base Camp verged on luxurious. With Passang in the kitchen and our Tibetan helper Kassang at his side, the menial chores, extending to laundry service, were all looked after. There was always more than enough pain higher up and alleviating any lower down kept us relaxed and ready to climb.

The lazy days of Advanced Base Camp were shattered by the requirement to get up at 2 a.m., eat as large a breakfast as morning nausea could handle, and stagger off in the pitch dark with a large pack, skis waving through the air, all to reach the High Camp below the North Face before the sun hit, melting the crevasse bridges and leaving the body in an oven of indefinable heat. The monsoon brought sunshine that reflected off the ice walls surrounding the glacier and turned the ascent into a fiery hell later in the day. I once recorded a temperature in the sun of 43 degrees Celsius, which makes long underwear feel like it is melting into the skin. The ascent from 5,000 to 6,200 metres took seven hours, with skis going on after two hours.

The crevasses of the glacier slid below the skis like curving snakes, lines of dark snow with barely perceptible ripples marking their depths. Skiing allowed a gentle rhythm, a swishing forward of the ski skins, passing through the ice towers overshadowed by the Himalayas rising on all sides, until the world below disappeared and life was only glacier and towering cliffs. The first climb up to High Camp was frightening, the crevasses unknown, slush avalanches sliding off the cliffs above. But the ski run down cleared the fear and replaced it with the exhilaration of the world's best slopes.

To stock the High Camp and get acclimatised, we'd be up and down seven times. But the conditions changed by the minute, a crevasse closed one day would be a gaping hole the next. The tent left at a halfway camp, when we had abandoned a carry in a blizzard, had been blown a kilometre away the next day by an unseen avalanche, only the trail of debris, ice chunks the size of lorries, to remind us we'd made the right decision in our hasty retreat. From a distance Everest looks like a quiet, immobile monster. But as we huddled directly at the foot of the face the clouds rushed in and out in blasts, the wind roared, storms came and went, snow dumped out of the sky at a metre every four hours and avalanches roared down like standing in the centre of Victoria Station in London. Then just as I nodded off to a troubled high-altitude sleep, the glacier would shift downward, the world moving with a groan and a crack, leaving me wondering if the next crevasse just might be opening up right under the tent.

Slipping on skis for the descent from High Camp caused the breath to hasten, the muscles to flex, the eyes to widen. On a good day the crust was crisp, a light overnight snowfall softening the surface, a slope no skifield groomer could improve on. The first drop, a rush of speed, every sense on edge, the crevasses filed in the brain and the angle they ran clicking forward to keep the skis at exact right angles. Edges cut into the ice, swooping through the corners, the powder flying up, cliffs flying past, dropping off into the steep roll of the glacier, tight turns through the icefall, dropping onto the lower expanse at high speed, coasting out around the corner and descending onto the glacial moraine. Twenty minutes of skiing focused every sense, every exhilaration, the combination of speed, control and a few life-threatening holes creating a complete break from the slower but more real fears of the climb up. Too bad it was five hours back up the hill through the gauntlet of killer avalanches and crevasses.

At the base of the North Face of Mt Everest is a series of bergschrunds, cliffs formed by the ice cascading down and the glacier pulling away into the Rongbuk Valley below. Most peaks are content with a single bergschrund, the definitive line between the mountain above and the glacier below. But on Everest, the ice cliffs roll and twist and extend up the ice face for 100 metres. Avalanches sweep over the bergschrunds, partially covering gaping holes.

On my first attempt, a 2 a.m. start had my ice axe still stabbing uselessly into the depths two hours later, ice tinkling away into the inky silence below, headlamp reflecting into the icy garden before shining off into infinite blackness. With the ice axe embedded in the upper edge, one giant step carried me up onto the Face. But two days later I was back, the Face having proved a morass of soft snow and miniature avalanches. I leapt onto the relative security of the glacier and proceeded back down on my skis.

The monsoon had provided waist-deep sugar snow, hugging the cliffs of the Couloir above my high point of 7,800 metres. My legs had become hidden appendages, the biggest challenge tunnelling upwards through the froth. So I returned with Mike to help break trail a few weeks later, climbing to 7,600 metres where we spent three nights battling blizzards and avalanches cascading over the tent roof, twisting the tent poles into an inverted umbrella. We finally escaped across avalanche-strewn slopes, onto our skis and into the mists of the glacier, melting back into the grassy meadows at Advanced Base Camp. The advantages of the monsoon — warmer temperatures, lower winds and the occasional brief window of fine weather — weren't materialising with any consistency. We opened another book, flipped over our tapes and blew some more air into our air mattresses. Patience was a virtue Everest forced upon us.

Unlike other Everest expeditions that have climbed en masse from Base Camp to the summit, we had been the only people in Base Camp and had moved on to spend over a month completely alone at Advanced Base Camp. Our friends were a herd of Himalayan blue sheep grazing outside the tent, fat and sassy snowcocks pecking grass, marmots chattering from the boulders and a lone lammergeier, the bearded vulture of the Himalayas with a wingspan of three metres, casting long shadows over the camp.

In mid-August we were joined by a group of Spanish (Catalan) climbers from Barcelona who became fast friends as we relaxed in the meadow next to their camp. Their doctor, Xavi Lamas, was doing research in Boston, USA, and with his easy command of English was particularly comfortable whiling away an evening with us. Several weeks after their arrival, they went on an acclimatisation climb of Changzheng, a 6,977 metre peak directly above camp.

'Robert?' the Catalan's Sherpa cook asked at my tent door a day later. 'Can I borrow your telescope?' They had called in on the radio — there had been an avalanche and they wanted him to look.

The avalanche path was obscured by clouds over 1,000 metres above. Having climbed the peak a month before, I remembered the avalanche track as it appeared from higher up, disappearing over cliffs into a hanging, cliff-strewn canyon. The next radio call confirmed only one thing — the climber who had been carried away was Xavi.

Mike and I climbed through cliffs to the base of the avalanche. The canyon was narrow, deep and dark, sun filtering down over the cliffs like rain. A single gorak, the pure black large raven of the Himalayas, carrier of omens both good and bad, hovered overhead. Xavi's ice axe lay in the snow at the tumbled base of an avalanche, a convoluted mass of snow blocks packed ten metres high and 30 metres wide. Next we saw his boot — but it was only a single boot, crampon still strapped tight. What violence would tear a tightly strapped mountaineering boot off a climber's foot?

We searched further above, the gorak circling lazily on the breeze overhead while the chill air of afternoon settled off the ice of the avalanche and into the canyon around us. Thrown out from the base of the avalanche, Xavi's body rested on the black rock and ice of the moraine, sloping steeply downhill. The avalanche had not been kind to him but after the first touch of his body, to slide him into the nylon bivouac sack, it became easier, practical problems overcoming our initial horror. I noticed we did not refer to him by name as we worked. Subconsciously we were taking our previously personal relationship with Xavi and putting it to one side.

We moved the body into a shallow icy groove on the glacier and covered it with rocks to protect it from the birds until we could return. Two days later we were back with the Catalan team for the funeral. A grave deep in the rocks was sunk as a final resting place, with the mountain he had fallen from behind him as a headstone and the expanse of the West Rongbuk Glacier at his feet. On a flat stone was carved in Catalan, 'Xavi Lamas. We will never forget you. 26 August 1995.' The wake back at Advanced Base Camp went on long into the evening, with the close-knit Catalan team reminiscing over past adventures.

Three days later Mike and I passed the base of the canyon where Xavi rested, on our way to the North Face. We'd never questioned returning to the mountain after his death, despite the brutal confirmation of the dangers. A body on our doorstep hadn't been predicted, but in a life of climbing, over the long run it wasn't entirely unexpected. Crossing the endless avalanche paths that ran below our ski tracks was done quickly and we pulled into Camp I at 6,500 metres in record time, just as the sun set.

The following evening, skis were strapped on at 9 p.m., stainless steel glinting in the light of the headlamps, snow crystals reflecting the flash of halogen bulbs. Outside the circle of the headlamps' reality, nothing existed. Skiing at night over hidden crevasses hopefully frozen solid, sliding uphill with the skis grabbing the snow with a gentle drag, was surreal. Hidden inside one-piece suits we were isolated from the cold, breath forming a fog cloud in the headlamps' beam. At the base of the first bergschrund, an ice cliff towering blue into the dark sky, the skis came off and the crampons went on, feet moving from sliding motion to crisp precision, biting into Everest like tiny teeth eating at the mountain. Ice tools edged us upwards through the night, crablike for six long hours until the dawn's grey. As the sun touched the West Ridge and spread its orange glow back across the Face, Camp II at 7,600 metres crawled into view.

At 4 o'clock the next morning the ritual was repeated. One head, then a second, popped out from the tent, like cartoon characters, and set off up the slope. We turned the corner into the Great Couloir and crabbed upwards. Unroped, we climbed independently, separate specks of identity connected only by footsteps linking our progress. The colours of the plateau over 3,000 metres below faded into brown, then blue, then finally pink. The altitude tunnelled the vision into a porthole of clarity, like looking directly from a plane window. Streamers of cloud stretched overhead, heralding the approaching storm. We kept climbing. We'd heard reports scratching in across the shortwave radio at Advanced Base Camp about the storm and seven deaths on K-2. Eight thousand metres allowed us only a snowflake of latitude in any decision. Xavi lurked in our thoughts, direct evidence that mountains were unkind.

At 8,000 metres a cliff band broke the side of the Great Couloir. A tiny platform of snow was glued to its side, room for our half-pint tent and a place to rest our feet. The snow level had risen from our knees to our thighs and progress had reached new lows. But

Seven Summits Solo — albeit now a duet — rested confidently: the thin air made the summit appear merely a hop overhead.

As darkness settled, snow began to fall and frost built up on the inside of the tent until it started snowing as much inside as out. Accustomed to the quietness of soloing, I found Mike's company especially welcome in the overwhelming solitude of Everest. We discussed coffee franchises, pizzas, and third world politics. Day floated into night, the weather bringing hope by day and blizzards by nightfall. Our one chance was to climb all night and into the next day to reach the summit; we weren't asking for perfect weather — just a low blizzard and perhaps some wind to blow a little snow away. After the second night, camping at 8,000 metres was losing its novelty and by the third evening we had to climb. Stove fuel, food and life itself were rapidly running out on us.

At 9 p.m. we exited the tent and entered the Great Couloir. The moon, a three-quarter crescent, curved over the cliffs at the far side of the shadowed canyon leading towards the summit. The moon arced through the jagged black cliffs, shining without reflection through the towers and cracks. A deep snowstorm whirled, circling, dropping into the apex of the Couloir. An eerie darkness pervaded everything, cut with moon-grey shadows. Only the outline of the cliffs was visible. The wind pushed the snow over the moon in waves, darkness lapping at reality. Our feet disappeared into the snowy darkness of the steep slope. Ice crept out of the crampons and up through our feet and into our legs. Our headlamps wavered upwards on the slope, the only sign of life. Snow crept up around our waists and rolled in gentle waves down the slope behind us, covering our tracks. The moon slid behind the Couloir like a ghostly friend exiting the room. Without a word we turned and slid back towards the tent. There would be no life above.

The retreat to Advanced Base Camp and on to Base Camp occurred in a post-high-altitude haze, the Catalans toasting both our highs and lows, happy to see us back alive again after we had disappeared into the clouds a week before. On the North-East Ridge, a Sherpa climbing with a Korean expedition was carried away by another avalanche and found dead under the snow half an hour later. As I walked down from Base Camp for his cremation, the day before our return to civilisation, the Buddhist belief that the soul wanders for 45 days after death whistled down the glacier in the wind. I felt light-headed from the days at 8,000 metres and the possibility that some part of me had died and the cremation might actually be my own. The rough wood stood gnarled and fresh next to the pyre. The body was tumbled out and a monk borrowed my knife to cut the man's clothes from his frigid body. His head fell back, it certainly wasn't me. My knife was handed to me, the fire blazed, the smoke rose into the sky and the gorak soared in lazy circles overhead. The summit of Everest was obscured by clouds, but it, like me, was still there, waiting.

Kathmandu, 19 September 1995

CONTINENTAL DIVIDE
by Glenn Porzak

On April 30, 1985, American businessman Dick Bass reached the summit of Mt Everest and became the first person to climb the highest peak on each of the world's seven continents (Africa, Antarctica, Asia, Australia, Europe, North and South America).

Controversy erupted, however, in August 1986, when Canadian Patrick Morrow reached the summit of Mt Elbrus and proclaimed that he, not Bass, was the first to climb the so-called 'seven summits'. Morrow had already climbed the 16,502-foot Carstensz Pyramid in the western half of New Guinea, and he asserted that this was the summit of Australasia — the true seventh continent. This alleged continent includes New Zealand, New Guinea and certain other Pacific Islands, along with Australia. If Australasia were truly a continent, Carstensz would replace the lowly 7,316-foot Mt Kosciusko (Australia's highest peak) as a continental summit.

The debate began in earnest in December 1986, when Reinhold Messner became the second person to climb Morrow's definition of the seven summits. Perhaps smarting from the fact that he was not allowed to join Bass's 1983 expedition to Mt Vinson, which would have given him the opportunity to be first to climb the seven summits by either definition, Messner sided with Morrow. The controversy was further fuelled when various adventure-travel companies saw the potential for profit in guiding clients up the technically difficult Carstensz. As there was no demand for a guided hike up Kosciusko, mountain guides quickly adopted Morrow's seventh-summit choice.

In 1992, I completed the seventh of the traditional seven summits; in 1994, I summited Carstensz — more out of intrigue with the mountain than from any feeling that Australia is not a continent. Having nothing to gain from either seven-summit definition, I would like to offer a few observations.

The first is based on plate tectonics. Morrow's premise is that New Guinea is part of the Australian continental shelf and plate. However, New Guinea does not entirely perch atop the Australian continental shelf. The island is a jigsaw of three plates that geologically contain Southeast Asia, the Southern Pacific and Australia. Only the island's low southern plains are part of the Australian plate. The Java Trench, which cuts through New Guinea, is the geological border that separates Asia from Australia. Carstensz Pyramid lies to the north of the mountain chain that marks the Java Trench, on the Philippine plate of Asia. Thus, it is not on the same tectonic plate as Australia.

My second observation looks at political classifications. Carstensz is located in the western half of New Guinea, known as Irian Jaya, which belongs to Indonesia. Politically, that country is classified as part of Asia, not Australia. Only eastern New Guinea, known as the independent country of Papua New Guinea, has any political ties to Australia.

Philosophically, Bass's claim also appears superior. Dick Bass defined the challenge to climb the continental summits. Then, as an inexperienced mountaineer in his mid-50s, he went out and did it. Perhaps that irritates some hard-core mountaineers, yet it shows what one can do with persistence.

Technicalities, politics and philosophy aside, two facts stand out. New Guinea is an island, and Carstensz is the highest mountain in the world situated on an island. Therefore, Kosciusko is the seventh summit. As the highest mountain in the world not located on a continent, Carstensz is surely the eighth.

Glenn Porzak is a past president of the Colorado Mountain Club and the American Alpine Club.

ACKNOWLEDGEMENTS

Major sponsors, who have helped make the pursuit of adventure and exploration possible:

Rolex Watch USA, Inc.
British Airways.
Kodak New Zealand Ltd.
Olympus Cameras.
SmithKline Beecham.

And sponsors who have assisted with products and enthusiasm for the Seven Summits Solo.

About Time: Christopher Grima.
Adventure Network: Anne Kershaw.
American Alpine Club: Phil Erard.
American Himalayan Foundation: Norbu and Terry Tenzing Norgay.
American Express.
Mads Anderson.
Bivouac: Wayne Martin.
Bibler Tents: Todd Bibler.
BMW: Geoff Fletcher.
Chinese Mountaineering Association: Ying Dao Shui.
Christchurch *Press*: Stan Darling.
Climbing Magazine: Michael Kennedy.
Clinique: Nathaniel Benson, Penny Thompson, Christine Duff.
David Bateman Ltd.: Paul Bateman, Tracey Borgfeldt
Joan R. Duncan.
Earth Sea Sky: David Ellis.
Ex Officio: Joseph Boldan.
Evening Post: Roger Foley.
The Explorers Club: David Swanson, Garrett Bowden.
Fairydown: Chris Bell, Steve Wilson.
Bill Forrest.

Dr Stephen Gilbert.
Peter Gillman.
Grainger & Associates: Tim Grainger, Stephanie Law.
Trevor Hall.
Stephen Haines.
Daryl Hughes.
Helly-Hansen: Brad Boren, Brian Leslie.
Inmarsat: Kevin Sullivan.
Meyer Home Center: Steve Schaefer.
Ron Moser.
Mountainsmith: Patrick Smith.
Mountain Travel-Sobek: Richard Bangs, Chuck Cross, Lynn Cross.
NBC: Tom Brokaw, Terry Byrne, Joe Witte.
New Zealand Herald: Gavin Ellis.
Ogilvy & Mather: Bill Phillips.
Olympus: Mike Bull, Alistair Boyd.
Outdoor Research: Ron Gregg, Monica Palmerton.
Pigeon Mountain Industries: Steve Hudson.
Raynish & Partners: Jenni Raynish, David Slack.
Rossignol: John King.
Joan, Brian & Craig Seddon, Barb Stringer.
David Sheppard.
Silver Oak Cellars: Ramond T. Duncan.
SmithKline Beecham: Mitch Cybulski, Vicki Glynn.
Sony.
Total Productions: David Watson.

And thanks to people who have shared information and support in the
mountains, the hills or maybe just in the pub:

Pete Athans, Conrad Anker, Bauer family, Mike Bearzi, Russ Belknap,
Chris Bonington, David Breashears, Jim Bridwell, Wade Calderwood,
Peter Cornwall, Wendy Davis, Hans-Christian Doseth, Tim Drisko,
Rob Dorival, Mike Duncan, Renee Duncan, Clive Duval,
Iver Otto Gjelstenli, Margaret Griffin, Bill Hammel, Mark Hesse,
Ang Kassang, Harry Kent, Nick Lydon, Scott Lee, Walt McConnell,
Reinhold Messner, Alexandre Morev, Warren Morgan, Passang Norbu,
Mike Perry, Steve Plumb, Miklos Pinther, Andy Politz, Pam Riley,
John Roskelly, Clay Sanford, Steve Sanford, Schaefer family, Paul Teare,
Paul Teten, Kassang Tsering, Jay Smith, Lars Stendal,
Mike and Betty Vlasek, Paul, Liz and Hannah-Jane Walters, Ed Webster,
Mark Whetu, Jim Wickwire, Sandy Wylie, Miriam Zieman.